So, You Think
You Know the Jersey Shore?

People, Places, Folklore, Trivia
and Treasures

By Maryanne Christiano-Mistretta

Omni Publishing Co.
2023

Published by Omni Publishing Co.
www.omni-pub.com

Cover Design: Dave Derby
www.DerbyCreative.com

Photos by Maryanne Christiano-Mistretta

Page 135, photos 1 and 2; Page 136, photos 3 and 4; Page 137, photos 5 and 6; Page 138, photos 7 and 8; Page 139, photos 9 and 10; Page 140 photos 11 and 12; Page 141, photos 13 and 14; Page 142, photos 15 and 16; Page 143, photos 17 and 18; Page 144, photos 19 and 20

Library of Congress cataloging in publication data

Christiano-Mistretta, Maryanne

So, You Think You Know the Jersey Shore?
People, Places, Folklore, Trivia and Treasures

ISBN: 978-1-928758-08-2

Author Information

Maryanne Christiano-Mistretta is an author, journalist, and motivational/public speaker.

Her latest books are *Be (Extra) Ordinary* and *I Don't Want to Be Like You*. Maryanne resides in New Jersey with her husband, Dennis, and their beloved cats. Aside from career, her interests include music, health, and spirituality.

Why I Love the Jersey Shore

I've been going to the Jersey Shore since I was a kid. Growing up in New Jersey, it's always been a special place for me. From family trips as a little girl, hitting the beach during the day and enjoying the boardwalk at night, to coming of age as a teenager. Hanging with my younger sister and other teens on the boardwalk gave you a sense of freedom, knowing that you were young and in a special place in life. Even well into my 20s, the Jersey Shore was an extraordinary place to be. Whether it was a day trip or a longer vacation, it was purely magical.

The beach is beautiful. There's nothing quite like a day spent on the beach at the Jersey Shore. With miles of clean beaches and crystal-clear water, you can spend hours swimming, sunbathing, or just taking in the gorgeous views.

But while it's nice to relax on the beach, the Jersey shore has so much more to offer. As you'll find in this book, there is absolutely plenty to do. Each shore town has its own bit of charm and personal identity. Anyone can find an area that is best suited for them; the Jersey Shore has something for everyone. And you don't have to take my word for it, come see for yourself!

-*Maryanne Christiano-Mistretta*

Introduction

The Jersey Shore has a rich history that dates back to the early 1800s when it was a popular vacation spot for wealthy families from Philadelphia and New York City. However, it wasn't until the mid-1900s when the area became more accessible to the general public, leading to the development of boardwalks, hotels, and amusement parks.

In the 1920s and 30s, Atlantic City became known as the "Queen of Resorts" and was a popular destination for famous figures such as Frank Sinatra and Dean Martin. As time went on, other towns along the shore also became popular vacation spots, including Wildwood, Seaside Heights, and Ocean City. These communities offered beautiful scenery, exciting attractions, and unforgettable experiences for families.

The Jersey Shore also played a significant role in World War II, serving as a training ground for troops and a site for submarine spotting. After the war, the shore experienced a surge in popularity as families flocked to the beaches for summer vacations.

The history of Jersey Shore is a fascinating story that has been unfolding for over two centuries. This iconic location has been a popular vacation spot for families since the early 1800s, attracting affluent visitors from Philadelphia and New York City. During this time, the Jersey Shore was renowned for its pristine beaches and beautiful landscapes, which provided a peaceful retreat for the wealthy.

This book celebrates all that is good in its history and the people and places of the Jersey Shore.

Table of Contents

The Jersey Shore

Jersey Shore was originally named Waynesburg by the two brothers, Reuben and Jeremiah Manning, who laid out the town circa 1785. Around the time that this was happening, a settlement arose on the eastern side of the West Branch Susquehanna River (Nippenose Township), opposite Waynesburg. A rivalry developed between the two settlements, and those on the eastern shore began referring to the settlement on the western shore as the "Jersey Shore," because the Manning family had relocated from New Jersey. The nickname became so fixed that in 1826 the original name of Waynesburg was officially abandoned and changed to Jersey Shore.

The Jersey Shore (known by locals simply as the Shore) is the coastal region of the U.S. state of New Jersey. Geographically, the term encompasses about 141 miles of oceanfront bordering the Atlantic Ocean, from Perth Amboy in the north to Cape May Point in the south.

The region includes Middlesex, Monmouth, Ocean, Atlantic, and Cape May counties, which are in the central and southern parts of the state. Located in the center of the Northeast Megalopolis, the northern half of the shore region is part of the New York metropolitan area, while the southern half of the shore region is part of the Delaware Valley, a.k.a. the Philadelphia metropolitan area. The Jersey Shore hosts the highest concentration of oceanside boardwalks in the United States.

Famous for its many boardwalks with arcades, amusement parks, and water parks boasting hundreds of rides and attractions, the Jersey Shore is a popular vacation spot with residents of North Jersey, New York, Maryland, Delaware, Connecticut, and Pennsylvania.

Certain shore communities are also popular with visitors of the Canadian province of Quebec. Due to New Jersey's peninsular geography, both sunrise and sunset are visible over water from different points on the Jersey Shore.

Hurricane Sandy in 2012 devastated much of the northern part of the region, spawning the demolition and rebuilding of entire neighborhoods, with reinvention on a physically and financially elevated and economically upscale level; this process of gentrification is rapidly escalating property values and transforming many communities on the Jersey Shore into a second home for the New York financial community, akin to the more established Gold Coast and Hamptons on Long Island.

The Monmouth House in Spring Lake opened its doors in 1876 and burned down in 1900.

All About Perth Amboy

Perth Amboy is a city in Middlesex County. Perth Amboy is part of the New York metropolitan area. As of the 2020 U.S. census, the city's population was 55,436. Perth Amboy has a Hispanic majority population. In the 2010 census, the Hispanic population made up 78.1% of the population, the second-highest in the state, behind Union City at 84.7%. Perth Amboy is known as the "City by the Bay," referring to its location adjoining Raritan Bay.

The earliest residents of the area were the Lenape Native Americans, who called the point on which the city lies "Ompoge." Perth Amboy was settled in 1683 by Scottish colonists and was called "New Perth" after James Drummond, 4th Earl of Perth; the native name was eventually corrupted and the two names were merged. Perth Amboy was formed by Royal charter in 1718, and the New Jersey Legislature reaffirmed its status in 1784, after independence. The city was a capital of the Province of New Jersey from 1686 to 1776. During the mid-1800s, the Industrial Revolution and immigration grew the city, developing a variety of neighborhoods which residents from a diverse range of ethnicities lived in. The city developed into a resort town for the Raritan Bayshore near it, but the city has grown in other industries since its redevelopment starting in the 1990s.

Perth Amboy borders the Arthur Kill and features a historic waterfront. The Perth Amboy Ferry Slip was once an important ferry slip on the route south from New York City; it was added to the National Register of Historic Places in 1978. The Raritan Yacht Club, one of the oldest yacht clubs in the United States, is located in the city. Perth Amboy is connected to the Staten Island borough of New York City via the Outterbridge Crossing.

People of Significance – Perth Amboy

Thomas Burnett Gordon (17 April 1652—April 28, 1722) was a Scottish emigrant to the Thirteen Colonies who became Chief Justice of the New Jersey Supreme Court and New Jersey Attorney General for the Province of New Jersey. He died in 1722 and is buried in St. Peter's Churchyard, Perth Amboy, NJ

John Watson (1685 – August 22, 1768) was an early American painter, born in Scotland. In 1715 he emigrated to Perth Amboy. Watson bought property in the city east of Rector Street and south of St. Peter's Episcopal Church on the Perth Amboy bluffs and built himself a house in which to reside and one to keep his paintings.

The New Jersey Historical Society has two portraits: one of William Eier, the first mayor of Perth Amboy, and one of Governor William Burnet. Watson died in 1768 and is buried in St. Peter's Episcopal Cemetery in Perth Amboy.

John Stevens Jr. (c. 1715 – May 10, 1792) was a prominent colonial American landowner, merchant, and politician. With his brother Richard, he owned mercantile vessels and commanded them on voyages to Madeira and the Caribbean between 1739 and 1743. He then settled in Perth Amboy, where he was a vestryman at St. Peter's Church from 1749 to 1752.

Do You Know – Perth Amboy?

The earliest residents of Perth Amboy were the **Lenape Native Americans** who called the point on which the city lies "Ompoge."

The area was dubbed **New Perth** in 1684 in honor of James Drummond who was an associate of a major Scottish proprietary and considered the Earl of Perth.

In 1684, **Perth Amboy** became the capital of East Jersey and remained the capital until the union of East and West Jersey in 1702.

The **Raritan Yacht Club** in Perth Amboy is one of the oldest yacht clubs in the United States.

In 1914, Perth Amboy had a baseball team called the **Pacers**. They only played for one season.

Local attractions include the Perth Amboy Ferry Slip, two small museums, an art gallery, a yacht club, and a marina.

Since 1939, legal use of a bicycle in Perth Amboy requires a license issued by the Perth Amboy police department.

Perth Amboy City Hall is the oldest in use in the United States.

Perth Amboy is usually regarded as the place where the first African American person, **Thomas Mundt Peterson**, voted (March 31, 1870) in the United States.

It is known for being the capital of colonial New Jersey from 1686 until 1776 and for its rich colonial history.

Perth Amboy is also famous for being the home of **naturalist John Audubon** best known for his bird illustrations, once resided in Perth Amboy and left a lasting impression on the city's vibrant ecosystem. And **geologist Henry Flagg Hatch** discovered the first dinosaur footprints in North America, also called Perth Amboy his home for a time.

Perth Amboy was designated as a **Historic District** in 1972 by the National Park Service due to its unique character and significant architectural resources. The sites within this district include several 18th-century wooden homes, Fort Stirling (the site of one of George Washington's battles with British forces), a train museum, Monument Square at City Hall Park and several other culturally significant landmarks.

Beyond its history and scientific heritage, Perth Amboy boasts a **diverse community** with a strong Latino influence. The city's downtown area features a variety of restaurants, bars, and shops that offer a unique blend of cultures and cuisines.

All About South Amboy

South Amboy is a suburban city in Middlesex County, located on Raritan Bay. As of the 2020 United States Census, the city's population was 9,411.

South Amboy and Perth Amboy, across the Raritan River, are collectively referred to as The Amboys. Signage for exit eleven on the New Jersey Turnpike refers to "The Amboys" as a destination.

People of Significance – South Amboy

Charles Pettit (1736 – September 4, 1806) was an American lawyer and merchant from New Jersey and Philadelphia, Pennsylvania. Pettit served as a personal secretary to Governor William Franklin from 1772 to 1774, and moved to South Amboy. As the Revolution neared, he resigned his post.

He returned to it in 1776 when appointed as secretary to the revolutionary governor, William Livingston. From 1776 to 1778 Pettit held the office of provincial secretary (a title specified by the 1776 New Jersey State Constitution and later known as Secretary of State of New Jersey).

Benjamin Franklin Howell (January 27, 1844 – February 1, 1933) was an American Republican Party politician who represented New Jersey's 3rd congressional district in the United States House of Representatives from 1895 to 1911.

Born in Cedarville, New Jersey, Howell attended the common schools, and graduated from Fort Edward Institute, New York. He enlisted in the Twelfth Regiment, New Jersey Volunteers, in 1862 and served until the close of the war. He engaged in mercantile pursuits in South Amboy, in 1865 and was named to the Township Committee, and served as Surrogate of Middlesex County from 1882 to 1892. He served as president of the People's National Bank of New Brunswick, vice president of the New Brunswick Savings Institution, and was a founder and vice president of the First National Bank of South Amboy (now known as Amboy Bank).

Richard Field Conover (November 20, 1858 – June 5, 1930) was an American tennis player, lawyer, and real estate manager. Conover was born in South Amboy, the son of Francis Stevens Conover and Helen Stockton Field. He was a grandson of Richard Stockton, a signer of the Declaration of Independence.

Do You Know – South Amboy?

Founded in 1798, South Amboy is located along the **Raritan River**, south of Staten Island and across the river from Perth Amboy.

Scenes from the 2000 film **"Coyote Ugly"** were filmed in South Amboy and the main character is from the city.

In 1932 **John Stevens** built the first railroad in New Jersey running between Camden and South Amboy.

The city was heavily damaged by military explosives in two major incidents. The 1918 explosions occurred during World War I at the Gillespie Shell Loading Plant, just south of the town. The 1950 explosion struck as Healing Lighterage Company dockworkers were transferring ammunition from a freight train onto barges. Both disasters killed dozens and injured hundreds of local victims, damaged hundreds of South Amboy buildings, required emergency declarations of martial law, and scattered wide areas of ammunition remnants that continue to surface occasionally.

All About Laurence Harbor (Old Bridge)

Laurence Harbor is an unincorporated community and census-designated place (CDP) located on the Raritan Bay within Old Bridge Township, in Middlesex County, New Jersey, United States. As of the 2010 United States Census, the CDP's population was 6,536.

People of Significance – Laurence Harbor (Old Bridge)

Edward Robert "Butch" Sanicki (July 7, 1923 – July 6, 1998) was an American professional baseball player. An outfielder, he appeared in 20 Major League games for the 1949 and 1951 Philadelphia Phillies. Born in Wallington, New Jersey, he attended Clifton High School, and threw and batted right-handed; he stood 5 feet 9 inches (1.75 m) tall and weighed 175 pounds.

He died on July 6, 1998, in Old Bridge Township and is buried at Holy Cross Burial Park, East Brunswick, N.J.

Joann H. Smith (May 12, 1934 - May 18, 1998) was an American politician who served in the New Jersey General Assembly from the 13th Legislative District from 1986 to 1998.

An Old Bridge Township member of the Middlesex County Republican Executive Committee from 1961 until her death, Joann Smith had also served as vice chair and recording secretary of the Old Bridge Republican Organization.

Smith served on the Old Bridge Township Zoning Board, and was a founder of the Old Bridge Economic development Corporation. In 1981 she was elected as a Republican to a four-year term on the Old Bridge Township Council, however this term was cut short as a result of the township's change from council–manager government to mayor–council government. Forced in 1983 to run for a new, four-year term under the

14

new form of government, Smith was narrowly defeated for one of three at-large seats.

Fabian Nicieza (born December 31, 1961) is an Argentine-American comic book writer and editor who is best known for his work on Marvel titles such as X-Men, X-Force, New Warriors, Nomad, Cable, Deadpool and Thunderbolts, for all of which he helped create numerous characters, among them Deadpool, Domino, Shatterstar, and Silhouette.

Nicieza was born in Buenos Aires, Argentina, the son of Omar and Irma Riguetti Nicieza. He was four years old when his family moved to the United States. Growing up in New Jersey, Nicieza learned to read and write from comic books. He lived first in Sayreville, New Jersey and moved to Old Bridge Township, where he attended Madison Central High School, from which he graduated in 1979.

Do You Know – Laurence Harbor (Old Bridge)?

The lands known today as Laurence Harbor were part of the south-ernmost region inhabited by the **Lenni Lenape tribe**, also known as the Delaware, in the 17th century.

Laurence Harbor is named after land developer **Laurence Lamb,** who bought property in (what was then known as) Madison Township at the turn of the 20th century and subdivided it into bungalow-sized lots.

Laurence Harbor was considered a beach resort back in the 1920s to 1950s.

Except for a few cold winter months, **great egrets** can be seen frequently in the area.

Along the boardwalk amongst the sand dunes, there are **honey-suckle trees** that blossom in the spring.

15

All About Keansburg

Keansburg is a borough in Monmouth County, in the U.S. state of New Jersey. At the 2020 United States census, its population was 9,755, a drop of 350 from the 2010 census enumeration of 10,105, in turn a decline of 627 (−5.8%) from 10,732 in the 2000 Census.

Keansburg was formed as a borough by an act of the New Jersey Legislature on March 26, 1917, from portions of both Middletown Township and Raritan Township (now Hazlet), based on the results of a referendum held on April 17, 1917.

It is part of the Bayshore Regional Strategic Plan, an effort by nine municipalities in northern Monmouth County to reinvigorate the area's economy by emphasizing its traditional downtowns, dense residential neighborhoods, maritime history, and the natural beauty of the Raritan Bay coastline.

People of Significance – Keansburg

James Paul Maher (November 3, 1865 – July 31, 1946) was an American labor union official, businessman, and politician. A Democrat, he is most notable for his service as a U.S. Representative from New York, a position he held for five terms (1911-1921).

After leaving Congress, Maher entered the real estate business in Brooklyn. He later moved to Keansburg, where he continued in real estate. Maher died in Keansburg on July 31, 1946. He was buried at St. Joseph's Cemetery, Keyport, New Jersey.

Frank Henry Field (February 27, 1922 – April 12, 2013) was an American chemist and mass spectrometric known for his work in the development of chemical ionization. He was born in Keansburg.

Eugene J. Bedell (May 13, 1928 – January 4, 2016) was an American politician who served in the New Jersey General Assembly from 1972 to 1974 from District 5B and in the New Jersey Senate from the 12th Legislative District from 1974 to 1982. He died on January 4, 2016, at his home in Keansburg at age 87.

Do You Know – Keansburg?

Keansburg was formed as a borough by an act of the New Jersey Legislature on March 26, 1917, from portions of both Middletown Township and Raritan Township (now Hazlet), based on the results of a referendum held on April 17, 1917.

In 1904 **William Gehlhaus** convinced five investors to join him in purchasing the area of marshland overlooking Raritan Bay in hopes of creating a resort area.

Keansburg is best known for its amusement park.

Question: What is the name of this amusement park?
Answer on page 18

All About Atlantic Highlands

Atlantic Highlands is a borough in Monmouth County, in the Bayshore Region. As of the 2020 United States census, the borough's population was 4,414, an increase of 29 (+0.7%) from the 2010 census count of 4,385, which in turn reflected a decline of 320 (−6.8%) from the 4,705 in the 2000 census.

Atlantic Highlands contains Mount Mitchill, the highest point on the eastern seaboard south of Maine, rising 266 feet (81 m) above sea level. The borough's name comes from its location overlooking the Atlantic Ocean.

Atlantic Highlands was incorporated as a borough by an act of the New Jersey Legislature on February 28, 1887, from portions of Middletown Township, based on the results of a referendum held that day. The borough was reincorporated on September 1, 1891.

Atlantic Highlands is part of the Bayshore Regional Strategic Plan, an effort by nine municipalities in northern Monmouth County to reinvigorate the area's economy by emphasizing the traditional downtowns, dense residential neighborhoods, maritime history, and the natural beauty of the Raritan Bayshore coastline.

People of Significance – Atlantic Highlands

Bernard F. Martin (February 4, 1845 – August 10, 1914) was an American politician from Manhattan, New York City. He died on August 10, 1914, at his summer home in Atlantic Highlands of "heart disease brought on by indigestion."

Answer from page 17: Morey's Pier in Wildwood

John Arthur Hall (September 16, 1877 – October 1, 1919) was an American football player and coach. He played college football for the Yale Bulldogs football team and was selected as a consensus honoree on the 1897 College Football All-America Team.

He also served as the head coach of the Carlisle Indians football team in 1898. Hall also played ice hockey on intercollegiate and amateur levels for Yale University and teams in New York City and Pittsburgh.

In September 1919, Hall was severely injured while driving from his summer home in Atlantic Highlands, to his winter home in the Sewaren neighborhood of Woodbridge Township, New Jersey. His automobile was hit by a train at a crossing in Keansburg. Hall's wife and mother-in-law were killed instantly, and Hall died the following day at a hospital in Long Branch, New Jersey. Hall and his wife were buried at the Evergreen Cemetery in New Haven, Connecticut.

Ruth Crawford Mitchell (June 2, 1890 – February 7, 1984) was the founding director of the University of Pittsburgh's Nationality Rooms in the Cathedral of Learning and had major oversight during the design, drafting and creation of the rooms between 1926 and 1956. She also raised the necessary funding for the project in addition to supervising architects and other contractors during the construction of the building.

She worked with immigrants in Pittsburgh and overseas committees to establish sponsorship of each classroom. Mitchell was a lecturer at the University of Pittsburgh in the Department of Economics. She led the project that resulted in the provision of support for foreign-born students at the University. Mitchell was born on June 2, 1890 in Atlantic Highlands.

Ernest Hemingway once said, "The world breaks everyone, and afterward, some are strong at the broken places." This sentiment is particularly poignant when considering the town's remarkable resilience in the face of adversity. Notably after its recovery from Hurricane Sandy.

Do You Know – Atlantic Highlands?

The Borough of Atlantic Highlands, once known as **Portland Pointe**, was originally part of Middletown Township. The major construction occurred from the 1880s through 1900. It included hotels, cottages, rooming houses, and private homes. Atlantic Highlands was a haven for bootleggers during the Prohibition era.

Atlantic Highlands Recreation Committee runs many events in town throughout the year including a Summer Concert Series in the harbor, youth programs such as basketball in the winter and soccer in the fall.

Atlantic Highlands' **Seastreak Ferry can** take you to Wall Street in 40 minutes.

Hurricane Sandy caused catastrophic damage to Atlantic Highlands. The storm destroyed all but 300 homes in the downtown area and claimed 150 of the 1500 homes in total. In addition, the town had to reject a sea wall project due to concerns about how it would affect the town. Superstorm Sandy was the largest Atlantic hurricane on record (by diameter), the second-costliest storm in U.S. history, affecting 24 states, and was responsible for flooding many homes and businesses.

Atlantic Highlands is also home to a **vibrant arts scene**, with numerous galleries and museums showcasing the work of local artists. From vibrant street murals to thought-provoking sculptures, the town is filled with creative energy and inspiration.

Atlantic Highlands is known for its beautiful landscapes and lighthouses, but it's also home to the famous quote "If you look close there is a bridge that my mom jumped off when she was a kid 'on a dare'!" This quote has been passed down through generations and is an iconic reminder of the adventurous spirit of Atlantic Highlands.

All About Red Bank

Red Bank is a borough in Monmouth County. Incorporated in 1908, the community is on the Navesink River, the area's original transportation route to the ocean and other ports. Red Bank is in the New York Metropolitan Area and is a commuter town of New York City. As of the 2020 United States Census, it had a population of 12,936, reflecting an increase of 730 (5.98%) from the 12,206 counted in the 2010 Census, which had in turn increased by 362 (3.06%) from the 11,844 counted in the 2000 Census. Red Bank is the fifth most densely populated town in Monmouth County.

Red Bank was formed as a town on March 17, 1870, from parts of Shrewsbury Township. On February 14, 1879, Red Bank became Shrewsbury City, part of Shrewsbury Township; this lasted until May 15, 1879, when Red Bank regained its independence. On March 10, 1908, Red Bank was formed as a borough by an act of the New Jersey Legislature and was set off from Shrewsbury Township. The borough was named for the red soil along the Navesink River.

Downtown Red Bank is notable for its many local and well-known businesses including Garmany, Urban Outfitters, and Tiffany & Co. on and around Broad Street. Many annual events happen throughout the year, including the International Beer, Wine & Food Festival, a long-running sidewalk sale, a farmers' market, an indie film festival, the Red Bank Guinness Oyster Festival, a Halloween parade, and a holiday town lighting.

People of Significance – Red Bank

Daniel V. Asay (June 26, 1847 – May 2, 1930) was an iceboat racer. He claimed to be the oldest ice yacht sailor in the world. His ice boat Gull competed in more races than any other in its class. He died on May 2, 1930, in Red Bank.

Timothy Thomas Fortune (October 3, 1856 – June 2, 1928) was an orator, civil rights leader, journalist, writer, editor, and publisher. He was the highly influential editor of the nation's leading black newspaper The New York Age and was the leading economist in the black community. He was a long-time adviser to Booker T. Washington and was the editor of Washington's first autobiography, The Story of My Life and Work. Fortune's philosophy of militant agitation on behalf of the rights of black people laid one of the foundations of the Civil Rights Movement.

Fortune moved to Red Bank in 1901, where he built his home, Maple Hall. The house was placed on the National Register of Historic Places on December 8, 1976, and the New Jersey Register of Historic Places on August 16, 1979.

Sigmund Eisner (February 14, 1859 – January 5, 1925) was a prominent manufacturer and president of the Sigmund Eisner Company based in Red Bank. At one time (1922), this company was the exclusive manufacturer of uniforms for the Boy Scouts of America and the largest manufacturer of uniforms in the United States. He is also known as the great-grandfather of Michael Eisner, who was CEO of The Walt Disney Company from 1984 to 2005.

Sigmund Eisner (and his family) took great interest in civic and social affairs. Sigmund was governor of the Monmouth Memorial Hospital and the State Home for Boys at Jamesburg, New Jersey. He was vice-president of the Red Cross of Monmouth County and water commissioner of Red Bank. He was a member of the American Jewish Committee, the Jewish Welfare Board of America, and the Zionist Committee of America.

His personal interests led him to membership in the Free and Accepted Masons, Ancient Order Nobles of the Mystic Shrine, the

Benevolent and Protective Order of the Elks and the Monmouth County Boat Club.

Do You Know – Red Bank?

Built in 1764, the **Sandy Hook Lighthouse** is the oldest standing lighthouse in the country.

Sandy Hook is home to **Fort Hancock**, a Nike Missile Base, and multiple hidden historical landmarks.

Cactus can be found on a Sandy Hook nature walk. You may also spot horseshoe crabs and seals.

Gunnison Beach in Sandy Hook is "clothing optional."

Question: Where is this lighthouse located?
Answer on page 24

All About Deal

Deal is a borough in Monmouth County, settled by Europeans in the mid-1660s and named after an English carpenter from Deal, Kent. As of the 2020 United States census, the borough's population was 900, an increase of 150 (+20.0%) from the 2010 census count of 750, which in turn reflected a decline of 320 (−29.9%) from the 1,070 counted in the 2000 census.

Deal boasts a significant population of Orthodox Sephardic Jews, mainly of Syrian origin. As much as 80% of Deal's population are Sephardi Jews, and the year-round population jumps ten-fold to over 6,000 during the summer, many of them Syrian Jews. In the 2000 Census, 16.4% of Deal residents identified as being of Syrian heritage, the greatest percentage of Syrian Americans in any municipality in the country. Most of the town consisted of homes close to or over one hundred years old in the Victorian and American Foursquare styles.

In 2007, Deal was ranked by Forbes magazine as the 13th most expensive ZIP Code in the nation with a median sale price of $1,825,000. It was also named the fourth most expensive zip code in New Jersey in 2017, with a median sale price of $1,207,500. In 2019, Property Shark ranked Deal in a tie with 94110 in San Francisco as the 85th most expensive ZIP Code in the country, and second-highest in New Jersey, with a median sales price of $1,500,000. Then again in 2021, it was ranked as the second most expensive zip code in New Jersey with a typical home value of $2,141,154. Then in 2022 it was ranked as the #1 most expensive zip code in New Jersey with homes valued at $2,400,000.

Answer from page 23: At Fort Hancock, Sandy Hook

People of Significance – Deal

Philip Hal Sims (November 8, 1886 – February 26, 1949) was an American bridge player. In 1932 he was ranked by Shepard Barclay, bridge commentator of the New York Herald Tribune, the second best player in the U.S. during the preceding year. (Barclay ranked Sims's regular partner Willard Karn first, the other two members of his Four Horsemen team third and fourth.)

In the 1930s, the Sims' resided in a home in Deal that was described in The Brooklyn Daily Eagle as reminiscent "of the castles of the feudal barons in medieval days."

Maxine Stuart (June 28, 1918 – June 6, 2013) was an American actress. Stuart was born in Deal as Maxine Shlivek, and raised in Manhattan and Lawrence, Nassau County, New York.

George K. Fraenkel (July 27, 1921 – June 10, 2009) was an American physical chemist, dean of Graduate School of Arts and Sciences and chairman of the chemistry department at Columbia University. Fraenkel was noted for his research of electron spin resonance. He also pioneered in the use of electronic techniques to study structures of molecules. Fraenkel was born on July 27, 1921, in Deal.

Do You Know – Deal?

Deal is a borough in Monmouth County, in the U.S. state of New Jersey, settled by Europeans in the mid-1660s and named after an English carpenter from Deal, Kent.

Eighty percent of Deal's population are **Sephardic Jews**.

In 2022 Deal ranked as New **Jersey's most expensive zip code** with homes valued at $2,400,000.

All About Oceanport

Oceanport is a borough in Monmouth County. As of the 2010 United States census, the borough's population was 5,832, reflecting an increase of 25 (+0.4%) from the 5,807 counted in the 2000 Census, which had in turn declined by 339 (−5.5%) from the 6,146 counted in the 1990 Census.

Oceanport was formed as a borough by an act of the New Jersey Legislature on April 6, 1920, from portions of Eatontown Township (now Eatontown), based on the results of a referendum held on May 11, 1920.

People of Significance – Oceanport

Charles W. Billings (November 26, 1866 – December 13, 1928) was a politician and competitive shooter from New Jersey who was a member of the 1912 Summer Olympics American trapshooting team that won the gold medal in team clay pigeons. He was a member of the New York Athletic Club. He competed in the Travers Island, New York clay pigeon shooting competition in both 1911 and 1913.

In 1912 he won the gold medal as member of the American team in the team clay pigeons' competition. In the individual trap competition he finished 42nd.

Billings, who had served from 1920 until his death as the first mayor of Oceanport, New Jersey, died of a heart attack on December 13, 1928, in Deal.

George H. Conway (c. 1878 – June 20, 1939) was a Triple Crown-winning American horse trainer who worked at Glen Riddle Farm in Berlin, Maryland. He is best known for training War Admiral, who won the Triple Crown in 1937 and was selected as the American Horse of the Year over his nephew and competitor Seabiscuit. Other notable horses trained by Conway include American Flag, who won the Belmont Stakes in 1925 before training with Conway, Crusader, who won the 1926

Belmont Stakes with Conway, Maid at Arms, who was the 1925 American Champion Three-Year-Old Filly, and War Relic, who was the last horse that Conway trained.

Conway retired to Oceanport, in June 1939, where he died on June 20, 1939.

Lewis Gustave Hansen (November 18, 1891 – November 18, 1965) was an American lawyer, judge, and politician who was the Democratic nominee for Governor of New Jersey in 1946.

Hansen served as Surrogate of Hudson County before retiring in 1957 to Oceanport. In 1965 he died in West Palm Beach, Florida on his 74th birthday.

Do You Know – Oceanport?

The land making up today's Oceanport was settled as part of the **Monmouth Patent**, a purchase agreement approved by royal Governor Richard Nicholls in 1665.

Oceanport is **a river town**, but throughout the 1700s, shipping was vital since the town had access to the ocean via the river it's on.

The town's fortunes improved when **Monmouth Park Racetrack** was opened in 1870 along the western side of town. Monmouth Park Racetrack is an American race track for thoroughbred horse racing owned by the New Jersey Sports and Exposition Authority and operated under a five-year lease as a partnership with Darby Development, LLC. Monmouth Park's marquee event is the Haskell Invitational, named after Amory L. Haskell. The Haskell was first run in 1968 as a handicap, but was made into an Invitational Handicap in 1981. It is now a 1⅛-mile test for three-year-olds run in late July. Monmouth Park also now showcases the Jersey Derby originally run at Garden State Park until its closure in 2001. The racetrack's season spans from early May to Labor Day in early September.

All About Long Branch

Long Branch is a beachside city in Monmouth County. As of the 2020 United States census, the city's population was 31,667, an increase of 948 (+3.1%) from the 2010 census count of 30,719, which in turn reflected a decline of 621 (-2.0%) from the 31,340 counted in the 2000 census. As of the 2010 census, it was the sixth-most-populous municipality in Monmouth County and had the 71st-highest population of any municipality in New Jersey.

Long Branch was formed on April 11, 1867, as the Long Branch Commission, from portions of Ocean Township. Long Branch was incorporated as a city by an act of the New Jersey Legislature on April 8, 1903, based on the results of a referendum, replacing the Long Branch Commission

People of Significance – Long Branch

Garret Augustus Hobart (June 3, 1844 – November 21, 1899) was the 24th vice president of the United States, serving from 1897 until his death in 1899. He was the sixth American vice president to die in office. Prior to serving as vice president, Hobart was an influential New Jersey businessman, politician, and political operative.

Garret Augustus Hobart was born in Long Branch, to Addison Willard Hobart and the former Sophia Vanderveer. Addison Hobart descended from the early colonial settlers of New England; many Hobarts served as pastors. Addison Hobart came to New Jersey to teach at a school in Bradevelt, New Jersey a small hamlet in Marlboro Township, New Jersey. His mother was descended from 17th-century Dutch settlers in New Amsterdam (today's New York City) who had moved to Long Island and then to New Jersey.

When Addison and Sophia Hobart married in 1841, they moved to Long Branch, where Addison founded an elementary school. Garret was born in Long Branch on June 3, 1844. Three children survived infancy; Garret was the second of three boys.

Hobart initially attended his father's school in Long Branch. The family moved to Marlboro in the early 1850s and he was sent to the village school.

John Webley Slocum (April 23, 1867 – May 22, 1938) was an American lawyer, politician, and judge. Slocum was born on April 23, 1867 near Long Branch, the son of Edward Randolph Slocum and Mary Jane Woolley.

Slocum graduated from the Long Branch High School in 1884, after which he began studying law with Judge Wilbur A. Heisley. He was admitted to the state bar as an attorney in 1888, and in 1892 he was admitted as a counsellor-at-law. He maintained a general law practice in Long Branch. He was appointed a Special Master in Chancery by Chancellor William J. Magie with the recommendation of Henry Stafford Little. He was president of the Long Branch Daily Record, the Long Branch Sewer Company, and the Independent Fire Company, as well as director and counsel of the Hollywood Land Company.

He was also president of the F. M. Taylor Publishing Company (which published the Long Branch Daily Record), vice-president and director of the Long Branch Trust Co., a member of the local board of education, and organizer and president of the West Long Branch Cemetery Trust. He served as Police Justice from 1889 to 1894 and City Solicitor from 1895 to 1900, at which point he resigned to focus on his law practice.

Slocum was a delegate to the 1912 Democratic National Convention. He was reappointed City Solicitor of Long Branch in 1906 and continued to hold that office when he was Senator. In 1911, he was elected to the New Jersey Senate as a Democrat, representing Monmouth County. He was the first Democratic Senator elected from Monmouth County in eighteen years. He served in the Senate in 1912, 1913, and 1914. He became President of the Senate in 1914, and in June of that year he served as Acting Governor when Governor James Fairman Fielder went on a western trip. After his term as Senator expired,

Governor Fieldner appointed him Judge of the Monmouth County Common Pleas Court.

He resigned from the court in May 1915 to accept an appointment to the Board of Public Utilities Commissioners. He became President of the Board in May 1918 following the resignation of Ralph W. E. Donges. He and the other three commissioners were removed from office by Governor Edward I. Edwards after a hearing in October 1920. The removals were sustained by the Supreme Court of New Jersey, and the commissioners brought the case before the New Jersey Court of Errors and Appeals.

In 1892, he married Ada Breece of Long Branch. They had no children. Slocum died at home from a heart attack on May 22, 1938. He was buried in the Slocum family plot in the West Long Branch Cemetery.

Clara Bloodgood (née Sutton Stephens; August 28, 1868 – December 5, 1907) was an American socialite who became a successful Broadway stage actress. She was born in Long Branch.

The Ulysses S. Grant Cottage was the Summer White House of **U.S. President Ulysses S. Grant** in Elberon, a part of Long Branch, New Jersey. Grant vacationed at the cottage starting in the summer of 1867, and thereafter spent three months of every summer there until 1885. He held cabinet meetings and composed parts of his memoirs at the cottage. The presence of Grant and the cottage helped popularize Elberon as a place for the elite to meet; a status that only faded when the railroad came to town, and it became more accessible. The cottage was demolished in 1963 by its then owner, who did not possess the funds necessary to preserve the building. The site is today a grassy field.

Do You Know— Long Branch?

Long Branch emerged as a beach resort town in the late 18th century, named for its location along a branch of the **South Shrewsbury River**. Long Branch takes its name from the "long branch" or south branch of the Shrewsbury River.

During its heyday in the 19th century, Long Branch was a resort town that for the **"Who's Who" of society.**

Seven Presidents Oceanfront Park is named for the first seven U.S. presidents who vacationed there. The park comprises thirty-eight acres and offers an ocean beach, swimming, fishing, boating, volleyball plus a boardwalk.

Long Branch's Pier Village is an award-winning mixed-use beach-front Victorian-inspired community which features over thirty notable restaurants as well as shopping.

Question: What is this a photo of?
Answer on page 32

All About Asbury Park

Asbury Park is a beachfront city located on the Jersey Shore in Monmouth County. It is part of the New York metropolitan area.

As of the 2020 United States census, the city's population was 15,188, a decrease of 928 (−5.8%) from the 2010 census count of 16,116, which in turn reflected a decline of 814 (−4.8%) from the 16,930 counted in the 2000 census.

In 2022, Asbury Park's beach was named one of the best in the world by Money and one of the best in the country by Travel + Leisure.

Asbury Park was originally incorporated as a borough by an act of the New Jersey Legislature on March 26, 1874, from portions of Ocean Township. The borough was reincorporated on February 28, 1893. Asbury Park was incorporated as a city, its current type of government, as of March 25, 1897.

People of Significance – Asbury Park

James Adam Bradley (February 14, 1830 – June 6, 1921) was a wealthy Manhattan brush manufacturer, financier, member of the New Jersey Senate, philanthropist, and real estate developer. He designed the resort destination of Asbury Park on the New Jersey Shore. Bradley was also involved in the development of Bradley Beach, which bears his name. Bradley served as the first postmaster of Asbury Park from 1874 to 1884, and established the city's first newspaper, the Asbury Park Journal (1876–1910), serving as its editor and proprietor until 1882.

Answer from page 31: A roof of an arcade in Asbury Park

Bradley began Asbury Park's first sewerage system in 1881 and set up water and gas works in 1884. Bradley also served as the first Mayor of Asbury Park, New Jersey (1893–1902) and as a councilman. In 1894, Bradley was elected to the New Jersey Senate from Monmouth County.

Charles Joseph "Charlie" (sometimes spelled "Charley") Kelly (February 18, 1859 – June 15, 1918), known professionally as **Charles J. Ross** or Charley Ross, was a Canadian-American entertainer, composer and theatrical producer who performed in vaudeville, burlesque, and on the stage. Ross and his wife, Mabel Fenton, became popular for their parodies of classical plays.

In the late 1890s, Ross and his wife opened Ross Fenton Farm, a resort hotel in Asbury Park that also doubled as their primary residence. For a number of years, Ross Fenton Farm was a popular mecca for New York area artist and entertainers. Most of the resort burned to the ground in 1950. Some of the original houses are still standing, including the main house of Charles Ross and Mable Fenton.

Ross died on June 15, 1918, at Ross Fenton Farm after a long illness and failed operation. Ross' wife Mabel died on April 19, 1931, in Los Angeles at the age of sixty-six. They are buried together at Glenwood Cemetery in West Long Branch, New Jersey.

Theodore Frank Appleby (October 10, 1864 – December 15, 1924) was an American Republican Party politician who represented New Jersey's 3rd congressional district in the United States House of Representatives from 1921 to 1923. He was the father of Stewart Hoffman Appleby, who also became a congressman from New Jersey.

Appleby served as a member of the Asbury Park, New Jersey Board of Education from 1887 to 1897, was a member of the State board of education from 1894 to 1902, was a delegate to the 1896 Republican National Convention, was a member of the city council from 1899 to 1906, served as Mayor of Asbury Park, New Jersey from 1908 to 1912, and was a member of the Monmouth County Board of Taxation from 1917 to 1920. He was elected as a Republican to serve as a congressman in the 67th Congress.

Do You Know – Asbury Park?

The town was founded in 1871 by **James A. Bradley**, a manufacturer from New York City and was named after Francis Asbury, the first bishop of the Methodist Episcopal Church in the United States.

Asbury Park was named for **Francis Asbury**, the first American bishop of the Methodist Episcopal Church in the United States.

In the 1920s, Paramount Theatre and Convention Hall complex, the Casino Arena and Carousel House, and two handsome red-brick pavilions were built in the **Asbury Boardwalk** area.

Asbury Park was the first Jersey Shore town to have a **municipal sewer system.**

In 1943, the New York Yankees held their **spring training in Asbury** Park instead of Florida.

The **Asbury Park exit** on the Garden State Parkway opened in 1956.

In 1965, **Margaret Hogan**, a former nun, opened the groundbreaking lesbian club, Chez Elle (French for "her house").

The **Stone Pony**, founded in 1974, was a starting point for many musicians.

After **Hurricane Sandy**, Asbury Park was one of the few communities on the Jersey Shore to reopen successfully for the 2013 summer season.

Visitors can enjoy great surfing on its endless sand beaches and find a revitalized Boardwalk full of things to do, including **The Stone Pony** which has been regarded as one of the world's most famous music "scenes" where Bruce Springsteen has made numerous appearances over the years.

It is known as the unofficial **gay capital** of New Jersey due to the gay community's strong influence. The gay community kick-started the revitalization in the early 2000's.

All About Ocean Grove

Ocean Grove is an unincorporated community and census-designated place (CDP) located within Neptune Township, Monmouth County. It had a population of 3,342 at the 2010 United States Census. It is located on the Atlantic Ocean's Jersey Shore, between Asbury Park to the north and Bradley Beach to the south. Listed on the National Register of Historic Places, Ocean Grove is noted for its abundant examples of Victorian architecture and the Great Auditorium, acclaimed as "the state's most wondrous wooden structure, soaring and sweeping, alive with the sound of music."

Ocean Grove was founded in 1869 as an outgrowth of the camp meeting movement in the United States, when a group of Methodist clergymen, led by William B. Osborn and Ellwood H. Stokes, formed the Ocean Grove Camp Meeting Association to develop and operate a summer camp meeting site on the New Jersey seashore. By the early 20th century, the popular Christian meeting ground became known as the "Queen of Religious Resorts." The community's land is still owned by the camp meeting association and leased to individual homeowners and businesses. Ocean Grove remains the longest-active camp meeting site in the United States.

People of Significance – Ocean Grove

Tali Esen Morgan (28 October 1858 – June 1941), born Taliesen Morgan, was a Welsh-born American conductor, composer, and publisher. He was the musical director at Ocean Grove, a large Methodist summer resort on the New Jersey shore, for almost twenty years.

Thomas Obadiah Chisholm (1866–1960) was an American hymn writer, poet, and Methodist minister. Towards the end of his life, Chisholm retired to the Methodist Home for the Aged in Ocean Grove. He died on February 29, 1960, in Ocean Grove.

Mary Porter Beegle, also known as Mary Urban, was an American dancer, theatre professional, and college administrator. She was born in Ocean Grove.

Do You Know – Ocean Grove?

On July 31, 1869, Reverend W. B. Osborn, Reverend Stokes, and other **Methodist ministers** camped at a shaded, well-drained spot, on New Jersey's seashore, and decided to establish a permanent Christian camp meeting community called "Ocean Grove."

Ocean Grove's Great Auditorium, constructed in 1894, is acclaimed as "the state's most wondrous wooden structure, soaring and sweeping, alive with the sound of music." Famed conductor, Leonard Bernstein once compared it to Carnegie Hall.

From May to September of each year, 114 tents are erected around the Great Auditorium to form "Tent City" a tradition of the **Camp Meeting Association** that dates back to 1869.

In 1975, Ocean Grove was designated a **State and National Historic District** as a 19th-century planned urban community. It has the most extensive collection of Victorian and early-20th century architecture in the United States.

Other **interesting facts** about Ocean Grove include:

- Until 1979, you couldn't drive in Ocean Grove on Sundays.
- Ocean Grove is a dry town. No liquor can be sold in Ocean Grove.
- Sabbath prohibits the driving of cars and trucks on Sundays.

All About Neptune Township

Neptune Township is a township in Monmouth County. As of the 2020 United States census, the township's population was 28,061, an increase of 126 (+0.5%) from the 2010 census enumeration of 27,935, in turn an increase of 245 (+0.9%) from the 27,690 counted in the 2000 census.

Neptune was incorporated as a township by an act of the New Jersey Legislature on February 26, 1879, from portions of Ocean Township. Portions of the township were taken to form Neptune City (October 4, 1881), Bradley Beach (March 13, 1893) and Ocean Grove (April 5, 1920, until the action was found unconstitutional and restored to Neptune Township as of June 16, 1921). The township was named for Neptune, the Roman water deity, and its location on the Atlantic Ocean.

People of Significance – Neptune

Isaac "Ike" Schlossbach (c. August 20, 1891 – August 1984) was an American polar explorer, submariner and aviation pioneer. He was born in Bradley Beach and raised in Neptune Township where he attended Neptune High School.

Haydn Proctor (June 16, 1903 – October 2, 1996) was an American politician and judge who served as President of the New Jersey Senate and Associate Justice of the New Jersey Supreme Court.

He attended Neptune High School, graduating in 1922, and Lafayette College, graduating in 1926. He went on to Yale Law School, where he was associate editor of the Yale Law Journal, earning his law degree in 1929.

Richard R. Stout (September 21, 1912 – October 16, 1986) was an American politician who served in the New Jersey Senate from 1952 to

1974. Born in the Ocean Grove section of Neptune Township, Stout attended Neptune High School, Lawrenceville School, Princeton University, and Newark Law School before becoming an attorney. He had also served in the U.S. Army during World War II from 1940 to 1946.

Do You Know – Neptune?

The Township of Neptune was named for the **Roman water deity**, and its location on the Atlantic Ocean.

Essex Road, which runs through Tinton Falls and Neptune, is known for tales of ghosts lurking in the woods.

Neptune City **had one church**, the Memorial United Methodist Church. As of 2023, the building was permanently closed and for sale.

Beach restoration following Hurricane Sandy

All About Avon-by-the Sea

Avon-by-the-Sea is a borough in Monmouth County. As of the 2010 United States census, the borough's population was 1,901, reflecting a decline of 343 (−15.3%) from the 2,244 counted in the 2000 Census, which had in turn increased by 79 (+3.6%) from the 2,165 counted in the 1990 Census.

Avon-by-the-Sea was incorporated as a borough by an act of the New Jersey Legislature on March 23, 1900, from portions of Neptune City. The borough was named for Avon, England, or for the Avon Inn, a hotel constructed in 1883.

People of Significance – Avon-by-the-Sea

Bronson Crocker Howard (October 7, 1842 – August 4, 1908) was an American dramatist. He died, aged 65, in Avon-by-the-Sea.

Edwin Donald Sterner (January 3, 1894 – September 30, 1983) was an American lumberman and Republican Party politician who served in both houses of the New Jersey Legislature and as chairman of the New Jersey Republican State Committee. He was also the first New Jersey Highway Commissioner.

A resident of Avon-by-the-Sea, he died on September 30, 1983 at the Jersey Shore Medical Center in Neptune City at the age of 89.

Mischa Levitzki (also spelled Levitski; Ukrainian: Міша Левицький (Miša Levycʹkyj); May 25, 1898 – January 2, 1941) was a Russian-born U.S.-based concert pianist.

Levitzki died suddenly of a heart attack aged forty-two, in 1941, at his home in Avon-by-the-Sea. Levitski's papers are conserved at the New York Public Library for the Performing Arts.

39

Do You Know – Avon-by-the Sea?

Avon-by-the-Sea was **incorporated as a borough** by an act of the New Jersey Legislature on March 23, 1900, from portions of Neptune City.

Avon-by-the-Sea is best known for its clean, white, sandy beaches. Year-round activities include boating and scuba diving.

Avon-by-the-Sea **can be revisited** in during off-season, as the non-commercial boardwalk is abounding with Victorian lamps, benches, and pavilions.

Question: What is this?
Answer on page 41

All About Belmar

Belmar is a borough in Monmouth County situated on the Jersey Shore. As of the 2010 United States census, the borough's population was 5,794, reflecting a decline of 251 (−4.2%) from the 6,045 counted in the 2000 Census, which had in turn increased by 168 (+2.9%) from the 5,877 counted in the 1990 Census.

What is now Belmar was originally incorporated as Ocean Beach borough by an act of the New Jersey Legislature on April 9, 1885, from portions of Wall Township, based on the results of a referendum held two days earlier. On April 16, 1889, it became the City of Elcho borough, which lasted for a few weeks until the name was changed to the City of Belmar Borough on May 14, 1889. The city acquired its current name, Borough of Belmar, on November 20, 1890. The borough's name means "beautiful sea" in Italian.

People of Significance – Belmar

Jay Patrick Lynch (January 7, 1945 – March 5, 2017) was an American cartoonist who played a key role in the underground comix movement with his Bijou Funnies and other titles. He is best known for his comic strip Nard n' Pat and the running gag Um tut sut. His work is sometimes signed Jayzey Lynch. Lynch was the main writer for Bazooka Joe comics from 1967 to 1990; he contributed to Mad, and in the 2000s expanded into the children's book field. Lynch was born in Orange, New Jersey and grew up Belmar, later moving to Florida.

Answer from page 40: Revolution Rail is a new outdoor adventure in Cape May where you pedal custom designed rail cars and ride on train tracks.

Douglas Crawford McMurtrie (July 20, 1888 – September 29, 1944) was an American typeface designer, graphic designer, historian, author and bibliographer of printing. He was born in Belmar.

Stephen L. Hoffman (born July 31, 1948) is an American physician-scientist, tropical medicine specialist and vaccinologist, who is the founder and chief executive and scientific officer of Sanaria Inc., a company dedicated to developing PfSPZ vaccines to prevent malaria.

Hoffman was raised initially in Belmar and subsequently in Ocean Township.

Do You Know – Belmar?

Belmar **mean "beautiful** sea" in Italian.

Belmar is known for **several annual events** including their Sand Castle Contest, their St. Patrick's Day Parade, their Pro Surf Contest, and their Sprint Triathlon.

Belmar is home to the **first and oldest** first-aid squad in the United States.

Belmar's "E" Street is the original source of **Bruce Springsteen's "E Street Band."**

In the HBO series, **"The Sopranos,"** Belmar is shown as the home port of Tony Soprano's boat, the Stugots.

American restauranteur, **Guy Fieri**, featured Belmar and local restaurant 10th Avenue Burrito in an episode of Food Network's "Diner's Drive-Ins, and Dives."

The Borough of Belmar's beaches and boardwalk **are open** on a year-round basis for swimming, sunning, fishing, surfing, boogie boarding and kayaking!

All About Spring Lake

Spring Lake is a borough situated on the Jersey Shore in Monmouth County. As of the 2010 United States census, the borough's population was 2,993, reflecting a decline of 574 (−16.1%) from the 3,567 counted in the 2000 Census, which had in turn increased by 68 (+1.9%) from the 3,499 counted in the 1990 Census.

People of Significance – Spring Lake

Robert Augustus Chesebrough, (January 9, 1837 – September 8, 1933) was an American chemist who discovered petroleum jelly—which he marketed as Vaseline—and founder of the Chesebrough Manufacturing Company.

Chesebrough lived to be 96 years old and was such a believer in Vaseline that he claimed to have eaten a spoonful of it every day. He died at his house in Spring Lake.

John Francis Crosby (October 26, 1889 – December 10, 1962) was an American attorney who served as the United States Attorney for the District of Connecticut under two presidents. He also served as the Assistant U.S. Attorney General. He died on December 10, 1962, at his home in Spring Lake.

Charles A. Agemian (July 22, 1909 – March 30, 1996) was an Armenian-American banker who took early retirement from Chase Manhattan Bank, where he was executive vice president of operations, to become chairman and chief executive officer of the Hackensack Trust Co., which later was renamed Garden State National Bank.

A resident of Spring Lake, Agemian died on March 30, 1996, at the age of eighty-six. He was married to Mary Agemian. They had two children: Sandra Borg and Mary Louise Heath.

43

Do You Know – Spring Lake?

During the "Gilded Age" of the late 19th and early 20th centuries, **Spring Lake** developed into a coastal resort for members of New York City and Philadelphia high society, in similar fashion to the settlements of Newport, Rhode Island and Bar Harbor, Maine.

This small beach resort area consisting of beautiful parks and Victorian homes is sometimes warmly called **"The Irish Riviera."**

Even during the summer's peak season, you will find very few people and almost no traffic in Spring Lake. **Even the long, non-commercial boardwalk is peaceful.**

Spring Lake's **downtown** is made up of upscale boutiques, cafes, and restaurants. There are no souvenir shops or chain stores.

The Borough of Spring Lake is one of the **smallest municipalities** in Monmouth County and covers only 0.45 square miles.

Spring Lake is home to some of the most beautiful homes in the state, including many historic **Victorian-style estates** built during the late 1800s and early 1900s. The Victorian-style estates in Spring Lake are some of the most magnificent homes in New Jersey and draw in visitors from all over the state. Many of these estates have been standing since the late 1800s and originate from the mid-1800s architectural movement known as "High Victorian Gothic."

In 2020, Spring Lake had **a population** of 3,000 people with a median age of 54 and an average household income of $136,075.

There are **seven public beaches** in Spring Lake that span over two miles along the Atlantic Ocean!

All About Sea Girt

Sea Girt is a borough in Monmouth County. As of the 2010 United States census, the borough's population was 1,828, reflecting a decline of 320 (−14.9%) from the 2,148 counted in the 2000 Census, which had in turn increased by 49 (+2.3%) from the 2,099 counted in the 1990 Census.

Sea Girt was formed as a borough by an act of the New Jersey Legislature on March 29, 1917, from portions of Wall Township, based on the results of a referendum held on May 1, 1917. The borough was named for the estate of Comm. Robert F. Stockton, who had purchased a property in the area in 1853.

People of Significance – Sea Girt

Robert Field Stockton (August 20, 1795 – October 7, 1866) was a United States Navy commodore, notable in the capture of California during the Mexican–American War. He was a naval innovator and an early advocate for a propeller-driven, steam-powered navy. Stockton was from a notable political family and also served as a U.S. senator from New Jersey.

In 1835, he purchased a property in Monmouth County, New Jersey, called "Sea Girt." The property was purchased in 1875 by a group of land developers, with the name of Stockton's estate ultimately leading to the choice of the name Sea Girt, New Jersey, when the borough was established in 1918.

Lawrence Aloysius Whipple (July 26, 1910 – June 8, 1983) was a United States district judge of the United States District Court for the District of New Jersey.

A resident of Sea Girt, Whipple died in nearby Red Bank, due to complications relating to heart surgery.

Frederick Bernard Lacey (September 9, 1920 – April 1, 2017) was a United States district judge of the United States District Court for the District of New Jersey.

On April 1, 2017, Lacey died in Naples, Florida at age 96. On April 17, 2017, New Jersey Governor Chris Christie signed an Executive Order directing that both United States and New Jersey flags at state departments, offices, and agencies be flown at half-mast on April 19, 2017, in recognition of Lacey's passing. A funeral mass was held for Lacey was held in Sea Girt where he had maintained a residence.

Do You Know – Sea Girt?

Sea Girt was named by **Commodore Stockton** after he purchased land in the area in 1853. But long before the white man settled in on this Jersey Shore spot, the Lenni Lenape Indians inhabited the area.

Sea Girt Light began operation on December 10, 1896, and is located on Ocean Avenue and Beacon Boulevard. It's one of four lighthouses left in New Jersey and offers stunning views from its observation deck.

Sea Girt's beaches and boardwalk **are open all year long**, with full time lifeguards on duty from Father's Day until Labor Day

One of the most famous quotes about Sea Girt comes from the book **"Sea Girt: A Brief History"** which reads: "Let the Summer Begin! We miss the summer when it's gone. That's why we can't help waiting impatiently for the summer to come again."

A popular event is **Sea Girt Day** which is held on Labor Day weekend. It's a family-friendly celebration filled with live music, games, crafts, food vendors, and more! Another highlight of this festival is the annual 5K & 10K run along the boardwalk - it's a great way to get some exercise while enjoying beautiful views of the ocean.

All About Manasquan

Manasquan (/mænəskwɑːn/, man-ə-SKWAHN) is a borough in Monmouth County. As of the 2020 United States census, the borough's population was 5,938, an increase of 41 (+.7%) from the 2010 census count of 5,897, which in turn reflected a decline of 413 (−6.5%) from the 6,310 counted at the 2000 Census.

The borough's name is of Lenape Native American origin, deriving from "Menschen" meaning "Place to Gather Grass or Reeds." Manasquan, Mannequin, Mannisquan, Manasquam, Squan, and Sequan Village are variations on the original pronunciation and spelling.

The borough's name has also been described as deriving from "Man-A-Squaw-Han" meaning "stream of the island of squaws," "an island with enclosure for squans," "island door" or "point/top." Manasquan, Maniquan, Mannisquan, Manasquam, Squan, and Squan Village are variations on the original pronunciation and spelling.

Manasquan was formed as a borough by an act of the New Jersey Legislature on December 30, 1887, from portions of Wall Township, based on the results of a referendum held the previous day.

People of Significance – Manasquan

Harold Charles "Hal" Thompson (October 18, 1922 – April 26, 2006) was an American football end and defensive end who played for two seasons in the National Football League (NFL). He played for the Brooklyn Dodgers from 1948 to 1949 after playing college football for the Delaware Fightin' Blue Hens. He was born in Manasquan.

Frank J. "Pat" Dodd (February 4, 1938 – May 14, 2010) was an American businessman and Democratic Party politician who served as President of the New Jersey Senate from 1974 to 1975. He resided in Manasquan.

Doris Burke (née Sable) is an American sports announcer and analyst for NBA on ESPN, NBA on ABC, College Basketball on ESPN, and College Basketball on ABC games. She formerly worked as an analyst for WNBA games on MSG, and has worked on New York Knicks games. Burke, the first female commentator to call a New York Knicks game on radio and television, was raised in Manasquan.

Do You Know – Manasquan?

The **Algonquin Arts Theatre** is a Manasquan landmark which has shown and movies throughout the year. It's a historic 540-seat theatre built in 1938 as a movie house and was converted to a professional live performance space in May 1994.

Manasquan was once a tourist destination and has turned into a year-round community due to the **demolition of traditional beach bungalows** and having lost many of the bars once located in its borders.

The **Firemans' Fair**, which dates back to 1974, with the exception of a decade-long hiatus from the late 1990s until 2011, occurs every July/August. The fair is the largest source of funding for Manasquan Volunteer Engine Company #2 and dates back to 1974. Though it was on a decade-long hiatus until the late 1990s, the five day-long festivities in 2011 were expected to draw 30,000 attendees.

Until 2010 Manasquan was home to the **Cat Fanciers' Association (CFA)**, the largest registry of pedigreed cats in the world.

The Manasquan Inlet provides surfers with waves that are corralled, refracted and enlarged by the jetty protruding out into the Atlantic Ocean. The Manasquan Inlet, reopened in 1931, is the northern terminus of the inland portion of the Intracoastal Waterway.

All About Point Pleasant Beach

Point Pleasant is a borough in Ocean County. As of the 2010 United States Census, the borough's population was 18,392, down from 19,306 in 2000 but still up from 18,177 in 1990.

The Borough is a Jersey Shore community situated south of the Manasquan River and north and east of the Beaverdam Creek and its confluence with the Metedeconk River.

Point Pleasant was incorporated as a borough by an act of the New Jersey Legislature on April 21, 1920, from portions of Brick Township, based on the results of a referendum held on May 19, 1920. The borough was reincorporated on March 12, 1928. Point Pleasant is distinct from Point Pleasant Beach, which is a separate community. The borough gets its name from Point Pleasant Beach, which gets its name from its location at the northern end of the Barnegat Peninsula, a long, narrow barrier peninsula that divides the Barnegat Bay from the Atlantic Ocean at the Manasquan Inlet.

People of Significance – Point Pleasant

Arthur Augustus Zimmerman (June 11, 1869 – October 22, 1936) was one of the world's greatest cycling sprint riders and winner of the first world championship in 1893. His prizes as an amateur were a consideration in the establishment of the International Cycling Association (ICA). Zimmerman stopped racing in 1905 and retired to Point Pleasant.

Eugene Gladstone O'Neill (October 16, 1888 – November 27, 1953) was an American playwright and Nobel laureate in literature. His poetically titled plays were among the first to introduce into the U.S. the drama techniques of realism, earlier associated with Russian playwright Anton Chekhov, Norwegian playwright Henrik Ibsen, and Swedish playwright August Strindberg. The tragedy Long Day's Journey into Night

49

is often included on lists of the finest U.S. plays in the 20th century, alongside Tennessee Williams's A Streetcar Named Desire and Arthur Miller's Death of a Salesman. In 1917, O'Neill met Agnes Boulton, a successful writer of commercial fiction, and they married on April 12, 1918. They lived in a home owned by her parents in Point Pleasant, New Jersey, after their marriage.

Agnes Ruby Boulton (September 19, 1893 – November 25, 1968) was a British-born American pulp magazine writer in the 1910s, later the wife of Eugene O'Neill.

Boulton was born in 1893 in London, England, the daughter of Cecil Maud (Williams) and Edward William Boulton, an artist. She grew up in Philadelphia and later in West Point Pleasant, New Jersey. She had married a Mr. Burton, who died prior to the meeting between O'Neill and Agnes Boulton; they had a daughter, Barbara. Boulton died on November 25, 1968 in West Point Pleasant.

Do You Know – Point Pleasant?

The Point Pleasant Beach area was first occupied by **the Lenape Native Americans**.

The Point Pleasant boardwalk spans a mile long and is made up of mostly amusement rides, the Jenkinson's Aquarium, pizza joints, ice cream parlors, games, and miniature golf courses. You can also find sushi.

Each September, **Point Pleasant Beach hosts** an annual Seafood Festival.

Point Pleasant Beach was one of the numerous Jersey Shore communities that was **devastated by Hurricane Sandy** in October 2012.

Composer Edward Manukyan, who lived in Point Pleasant Beach briefly wrote the song "Point Pleasant Beach" about the borough.

All About Seaside Heights

Seaside Heights is a borough in Ocean County. As of the 2020 U.S. census, the borough's population was 2,887, reflecting a decline of 268 (−8.5%) from the 3,155 counted in the 2000 census, which had in turn increased by 789 (+33.3%) from the 2,366 counted in the 1990 census. Seaside Heights is situated on the Barnegat Peninsula, a long, narrow barrier peninsula that separates Barnegat Bay from the Atlantic Ocean. During the summer, the borough attracts a crowd under the age of twenty-one, drawn to a community with boardwalk entertainment and one of the few shore communities with sizable numbers of apartments, attracting as many as 65,000 people who are often out until early morning visiting bars and restaurants.

Based on the results of a referendum held on March 25, 1913, Seaside Heights was incorporated as a borough by an act of the New Jersey Legislature on February 26, 1913, from portions of both Berkeley Township and Dover Township (now Toms River Township). The borough was named for its location on the Atlantic Ocean.

As a resort community, the beach, an amusement-oriented boardwalk, and numerous clubs and bars, make it a popular destination. Seaside Heights calls itself, "Your Home for Family Fun Since 1913!" The beach season runs from March to October, with the peak months being July and August, when the summer population explodes to 30,000 to 65,000. Route 37 in Toms River is routinely gridlocked on Friday afternoons in the summer months as vacationers travel to the barrier islands. The community is also known as the location of the hit MTV show Jersey Shore, with the director of the borough's business improvement district saying in 2010 that "we can't even calculate the economic benefit" to Seaside Heights from the continued presence of the show.

People of Significance – Seaside Heights

Fred L. Ashton, Jr. (March 7, 1931 – May 9, 2013) was an American politician who served as the mayor of Easton, Pennsylvania, from 1968 to 1976. Ashton also served as the first strong mayor of Easton, beginning with his inauguration for a second term in 1972. He was a member of the Republican Party.

Ashton lived in Seaside Heights after leaving local politics. He and his wife were licensed brokers at Crossroads Realty in Lavallette, before his retirement.

He had been living with his sister since Hurricane Sandy damaged his own Seaside Heights home in October 2012. Ashton died at his sister's residence, in the Easton, Pennsylvania area, on May 9, 2013, at the age of eighty-two.

Lou Taylor Pucci (born July 27, 1985) is an American actor who first appeared on film in Rebecca Miller's Personal Velocity: Three Portraits in 2002. Pucci had his breakthrough leading role in Thumbsucker (2005), for which he won a Special Jury Prize at the Sundance Film Festival and the Silver Bear for Best Actor at the Berlin Film Festival. Pucci then starred in The Chumscrubber (2005), Fast Food Nation (2006), The Go-Getter (2007), Explicit Ills (2008), and Carriers (2009). Pucci had starring roles in the 2013 Evil Dead remake, as well as The Story of Luke (2013) and Spring (2014). Pucci was born in Seaside Heights.

Do You Know – Seaside Heights?

Seaside Heights is a resort community, **made popular** by the beach, an amusement-oriented boardwalk, and numerous bars and clubs.

Seaside Heights is known as the location of the MTV hit show, **"Jersey Shore"** which was an economic benefit to the town, according to the director of the borough's business improvement district.

The two boardwalk amusement park piers at Seaside Heights are **Casino Pier** and **Funtown Pier**. They offer many family-friendly attractions ranging from arcades to games of chance, to beaches, and to the wide variety of foods and desserts, all within walking distance.

In 1985 New Jersey rock band **Bon Jovi** filmed most of their music video for the song, "In and Out of Love" in Seaside Heights, on the boardwalk.

The ABC soap opera, **"One Life to Live"** filmed a portion of its 2008 storyline in Seaside Heights, mainly on the beach and boardwalk.

In the summer at Seaside Heights, there **is free seaside entertainment** which includes movies on the beach, concerts, and weekly fireworks displays.

Seaside Heights is noted for their annual **Polar Bear Plunge**, where swimmers go into the icy cold Atlantic during winter in order to raise money for the Special Olympics.

In 1915, Senate Amusement Company of Philadelphia planned to build an ocean-side attraction in Seaside Heights within feet of the border to Seaside Park. Their plan was to build a covered pier to house a carousel. The structure was built in 1915 under the direction of Joseph Vanderslice of Senate Amusement Company. Budget issues stalled the project in 1916, and the amusement ride and building was subsequently sold to Frank Freeman. The combination of the completion of the Toms River Bridge on October 23, 1914 and the DuPont Avenue carousel and boardwalk are what likely led to the 159% population growth shown between the 1920 and 1930 censuses in Seaside Heights.

All About Toms River

Toms River is a township in Ocean County. Its mainland portion is also a census-designated place of the same name, which serves as the county seat of Ocean County. Formerly known as the Township of Dover, in 2006 voters approved a change of the official name to the Township of Toms River, adopting the name of the largest unincorporated community within the township. Located at the heart of the Jersey Shore region, the township is a bedroom suburb of New York City in the New York metropolitan area and a regional commercial hub in central New Jersey.

As of the 2020 U.S. census, the township had a total population of 95,438, with the township ranking as the eighth-most-populous municipality in the state in 2020, the same ranking as 2010 and the second most-populous municipality in Ocean County behind Lakewood Township, which had a population of 135,158. The 2020 population increased by 4,199 (+4.6%) from the 91,239 counted in the 2010 Census, which had in turn increased by 1,533 (+1.7%) from the 89,706 counted in the 2000 census. Toms River is featured in various TV and news media, including MTV's Made and Jersey Shore (seasons 1, 3, and 5), HBO's Boardwalk Empire and the original The Amityville Horror movie. In 1998, Toms River East Little League won the Little League World Series. The township has what is said to be the second-largest Halloween parade in the world.

In 2006, Toms River was ranked by Morgan Quitno Press as the 15th safest city in the United States, of 369 cities nationwide. In 2007, Toms River was again ranked as the 14th-safest city in the United States of 371 cities nationwide.

People of Significance – Toms River

Platt Adams (March 23, 1885 – February 27, 1961) was an American athlete. He competed in various events at the 1908 and 1912 Olympics and won a gold and a silver medal in jumping events in 1912. He died at his home in the Normandy Beach section of Toms River, New Jersey on February 27, 1961.

Marguerite de Angeli (March 14, 1889 – June 16, 1987) was an American writer and illustrator of children's books including the 1950 Newbery Award winning book The Door in the Wall. She wrote and illustrated twenty-eight of her own books and illustrated more than three dozen books and numerous magazine stories and articles for other authors.

In 1908, she met John Dailey de Angeli, a violinist, known as Dai. They were married in Toronto on April 12, 1910. The first of their six children, John Shadrach de Angeli, was born one year later. After living in many locations in the American and Canadian West, they settled in the Philadelphia suburb of Collingswood, New Jersey. There, in 1921, Marguerite started to study drawing under her mentor, Maurice Bower. In 1922, Marguerite began illustrating a Sunday School paper and was soon doing illustrations for magazines such as The Country Gentleman, Ladies' Home Journal, and The American Girl, besides illustrating books for authors including Helen Ferris, Elsie Singmaster, Cornelia Meigs, and Dorothy Canfield Fisher. Her last child, Maurice Bower de Angeli, was born in 1928, seven years before the 1935 publication of her first book, Ted and Nina Go to the Grocery Store.

The de Angeli family moved frequently, returning to Pennsylvania and living north of Philadelphia in Jenkintown, west of Philadelphia in the Manoa neighborhood of Havertown, on Carpenter Lane in Germantown, Philadelphia, on Panama Street in Center City, Philadelphia, in an apartment near the Philadelphia Museum of Art, and in a cottage in Green Lane, Pennsylvania. They also maintained a summer cabin on Money Island in Toms River. Marguerite's husband died in 1969, eight months before their 60th wedding anniversary.

Alf Goullet (5 April 1891 – 11 March 1995) was an Australian cyclist who won more than 400 races on three continents, including 15 six-day races. He set world records from two-thirds of a mile to 50 miles, and the record for the distance ridden in a six-day race.

Do You Know – Toms River?

European settlers first arrived in the area between 1614 and 1685. In 1685, the British-born **Thomas Luker** settled along the banks of what was then called Goose Creek. Luker began operating a small ferry service across the waterway, eventually becoming known as Toms River.

Joshua Huddy Park is located in Downtown Toms River and is host to a replica constructed in 1931 of the Revolutionary War fort that was once standing near the site.

Toms River is **featured in various TV** and news media, including MTV's "Made" and "Jersey Shore," HBO's "Boardwalk Empire" and the original "The Amityville Horror" movie.

In 1998 Toms River East Little League won the **Little League World Series**.

Toms River has the **second-largest Halloween parade** in the world.

Toms River **has many shopping malls** including Ocean County Mall, the only enclosed mall in Ocean County and the Seacourt Pavilion, located across Bay Avenue from the Ocean County Mall.

The **Lenni Lenape** (Original People) were the first residents of the area that became Toms River, occupying the land for thousands of years.

In 1782, British troops attacked the town of Toms River during the American Revolutionary War, quickly taking the lightly guarded salt works and blockhouse and destroying nearly every building in the town. The British also laid siege to a blockhouse that was manned by 25 militiamen who were committed to the cause of independence. This battle, known as the **Toms River Blockhouse Fight**, caused peace negotiations with Great Britain to come to a standstill.

All About Bay Head

Bay Head is a borough in Ocean County. As of the 2010 United States Census, the borough's population was 968, reflecting a decline of 270 (−21.8%) from the 1,238 counted in the 2000 Census, which had in turn increased by 12 (+1.0%) from the 1,226 counted in the 1990 Census.

Bay Head is situated on the Barnegat Peninsula, also known as Barnegat Bay Island, a long, narrow barrier island that separates Barnegat Bay from the Atlantic Ocean. Together with Mantoloking, Bay Head is considered part of the Jersey Shore's "Gold Coast."

Bay Head was incorporated as a Borough by an act of the New Jersey Legislature on June 15, 1886, from portions of Brick Township, based on the results of a referendum held three days earlier.

The community was supposed to have been named "Bayhead" after the Bayhead Land Company that developed the area in the 1870s. A railroad sign posted in the 1880s labeled the station as "Bay Head," and the name stuck when the borough was incorporated in 1886. The name also comes from the town's location, which is at the "head" of Barnegat Bay.

People of Significance – Bay Head

John Wanamaker (July 11, 1838 – December 12, 1922) was an American merchant and religious, civic, and political figure, considered by some to be a proponent of advertising and a "pioneer in marketing." He was born in Philadelphia and served as U.S. Postmaster General during the term of U.S. President Benjamin Harrison from 1889 to 1893.

He owned homes in Philadelphia, Cape May Point, and Bay Head, New York City, Florida, London, Paris, and Biarritz.

James C. Kellogg III (1915–1980) was Chairman of the Port Authority of New York & New Jersey and chairman of the Board of Governors of the New York Stock Exchange. He was a longtime resident of Elizabeth and Bay Head, New Jersey and was active in local affairs.

Dean Cetrulo (February 24, 1919 – May 9, 2010) was an American fencer. He won a bronze medal in the team sabre event at the 1948 Summer Olympics. He died in Bay Head at the age of ninety-one.

Do You Know – Bay Head?

The **Bayhead Land Company** was incorporated on September 6, 1879, capitalized at $12,000. The founding partners of Bay Head were David H. Mount of Rocky Hill, and three Princeton men: Edward Howe, his brother Leavitt Howe and William Harris.

Bay Head's **historic district** is architecturally significant for its large collection of well-preserved Shingle Style, Stick Style, and Queen Anne Style structures.

Bay Head is **less than a square mile** and everything is within walking distance—the beach, restaurants, a wine and cheese shop, a bakery, public tennis courts, gift shops, bed and breakfasts, and a bank.

Bay Head has **no bars, nor a commercial boardwalk.**

In the 2013 gubernatorial election, Republican Chris Christie received 80.4% of the vote (370 cast), ahead of Democrat Barbara Buono with 17.8% (82 votes), and other candidates with 1.7% (8 votes), among the 471 ballots cast by the borough's 838 registered voters (11 ballots were spoiled), for a turnout of 56.2% In the 2009 gubernatorial election, Republican Chris Christie received 70.3% of the vote (392 ballots cast), ahead of Democrat Jon Corzine with 22.2% (124 votes), Independent Chris Daggett with 6.3% (35 votes) and other candidates with 0.5% (3 votes), among the 558 ballots cast by the borough's 868 registered voters, yielding a 64.3% turnout.

All About Atlantic City

Atlantic City, sometimes referred to by its initials A.C., is a coastal resort city in Atlantic County. The city is known for its casinos, boardwalk, and beaches.

As of the 2020 census, the city had a population of 38,497, a decline of 1,061 (-2.7%) from the 2010 census count of 39,558. Atlantic City and Hammonton are the two principal cities of the Atlantic City-Hammonton metropolitan statistical area, which encompasses those cities and all of Atlantic County for statistical purposes and are part of the Delaware Valley metropolitan area, the nation's seventh-largest metropolitan area with 6.228 million people as of 2020.

The city was incorporated on May 1, 1854, from portions of Egg Harbor Township and Galloway Township. It is located on Absecon Island and borders Absecon, Brigantine, Egg Harbor Township, Galloway Township, Pleasantville, Ventnor City, and the Atlantic Ocean.

Atlantic City inspired the U.S. version of the board game Monopoly, which uses various Atlantic City street names and destinations in the game. Since 1921, Atlantic City has been the home of the Miss America pageant. In 1976, New Jersey voters legalized casino gambling in Atlantic City, and the first casino opened in 1978.

People of Significance – Atlantic City

John James Gardner (October 17, 1845 – February 7, 1921) was an American Republican Party politician who represented New Jersey's 2nd congressional district in the United States House of Representatives for ten terms from 1893 to 1913, and was Mayor of Atlantic City, New Jersey.

Born in Atlantic County, Gardner attended the common schools and the University of Michigan Law School in 1866 and 1867. He served in the 6th New Jersey Volunteer Infantry from 1861 to 1865 and one year in the United States Veteran Volunteers. He engaged in the real estate and insurance business.

Gardner was elected alderman of Atlantic City in 1867. He served as Mayor of Atlantic City, New Jersey in 1868 to 1872 and again from 1874 to 1875.

He died of heart disease at his farm in Indian Mills in Shamong Township, New Jersey on February 7, 1921 and was interred in Atlantic City Cemetery in Pleasantville, New Jersey.

Isaac Bacharach (January 5, 1870 – September 5, 1956) was an American Republican Party politician from New Jersey who represented the 2nd congressional district from 1915 to 1937.

He served as member of the council of Atlantic City from 1905 to 1910, and served as a member of the New Jersey General Assembly in 1911. His brother, Harry Bacharach, was also involved in Atlantic City politics and served several terms as mayor.

After leaving Congress, he engaged in the real-estate and insurance business in Atlantic City until his death there on September 5, 1956.

Edward Lawrence Bader (June 8, 1874 – January 29, 1927) was an American politician who served as Mayor of Atlantic City, New Jersey for much of the Roaring Twenties, when the city was arguably at the peak of its popularity as a vacation spot. Bader was known for his contributions to the construction, athletics, and aviation of Atlantic City.

Do You Know – Atlantic City?

Atlantic City was incorporated in 1854, the same year train service began on the **Camden and Atlantic Railroad**.

The **Atlantic City Boardwalk** was built in 1870 along a portion of the beach in an effort to help hotel owners keep sand out of their lobbies.

In 1883 salt-water taffy was conceived in Atlantic City by David Bradley.

Atlantic City, **sometimes referred to** by its initials A.C., is a coastal resort city in Atlantic County. It's known for its casinos, boardwalk, and beaches.

Atlantic City inspired the U.S. version of the board game **Monopoly,** which uses various Atlantic City street names and destinations in the game.

Since 1921 Atlantic City has been the **home of the Miss American** pageant.

In 1976 New Jersey voters **legalized casino gambling** in Atlantic City, and the first casino opened in 1978.

Notable Atlantic City **attractions** include the Boardwalk Hall, House of Blues, and the famous Ripley's Believe It or Not museum.

Atlantic City Boardwalk

All About Ventnor City

Ventnor City is a city in Atlantic County. As of the 2020 United States census, the city's population was 9,210, a decrease of 1,440 in the preceding decade. As of the 2010 U.S. census, the city's population was 10,650, reflecting a decrease of 2,260 (−17.5%) from the 12,910 counted in the 2000 census, which had in turn increased by 1,905 (+17.3%) from the 11,005 counted in the 1990 census.[22]

Ventnor City was incorporated as a city by an act of the New Jersey Legislature on March 17, 1903, from portions of Egg Harbor Township.

People of Significance – Ventnor City

Siegmund Lubin (born Zygmunt Lubszyński, April 20, 1851 – September 11, 1923) was an American motion picture pioneer who founded the Lubin Manufacturing Company (1902–1917) of Philadelphia. He died on September 11, 1923, at his home in Ventnor.

Walter Evans Edge (November 20, 1873 – October 29, 1956) was an American diplomat and Republican politician who served as the 36th governor of New Jersey, from 1917 to 1919 and again from 1944 to 1947, during both World War I and World War II. Edge also served as United States Senator representing New Jersey from 1919 to 1929 and as United States Ambassador to France from 1929 to 1933.

In the early 1920s Edge lived in a cottage on States Avenue in Atlantic City that was near the Boardwalk. In 1923, he moved to a new beachfront home in Ventnor that was located between Oxford and Somerset Avenues. This was his official residence until the mid-1940s, and thereafter was used by him as a summer home.

Geoff Pierson portrayed him in HBO's Boardwalk Empire.

Sol S. Metzger (December 29, 1880 – January 18, 1932) was an American football player, coach of football and basketball, college athletics administrator, and sports journalist. He served as the head football coach at Baylor University (1904), the University of Pennsylvania (1908), Oregon State University (1909), West Virginia University (1914–1915), Washington & Jefferson College (1916–1917), Union College (1919), the University of South Carolina (1920–1924).

Metzger was also the head basketball coach at South Carolina for one season in 1920–21, tallying a mark of 7–11. In addition, Metzger wrote a nationally syndicated sports column. A resident of Ventnor City, he died there on January 18, 1932, of erysipelas developed after surgery.

Do You Know – Ventnor City?

Ventnor City it takes its name from another seaside resort in England.

Ventnor City was among the first communities in the United States to be developed as an automobile suburb, a community that was developed for people who owned cars.

The **Ventnor City Boardwalk** is one of the Jersey Shore's gems that offers an amazing view of the Atlantic Ocean.

The **Great Ventnor City Fire of 1923** is a famous fire that occurred on the beach in Ventnor City, New Jersey. On August 8th, 1923, a fire broke out in a hotel on the boardwalk and quickly spread to other buildings due to strong winds. The fire destroyed over 100 buildings, including hotels, stores and homes. It also caused extensive damage to the boardwalk and amusement park.

The cause of the fire was never determined but it is believed to have been started by an electrical short circuit or a discarded cigarette butt. Despite the efforts of firefighters from nearby towns, the fire could not be contained and it burned for hours before finally being extinguished.

All About Brigantine

Brigantine (or simply The Island) is a city in Atlantic County. As of the 2020 United States Census, the city's population was 7,716, a decrease of 1,734 (−18.3%) from the 2010 census count of 9,450, which in turn reflected a decline of 3,144 (−25.0%) from the 12,594 counted in the 2000 census.

What is now the City of Brigantine has passed through a series of names and re-incorporations since it was first created. The area was originally incorporated as Brigantine Beach Borough by an act of the New Jersey Legislature on June 14, 1890, from portions of Galloway Township, based on the results of a referendum held on June 3, 1890. On April 23, 1897, the area was reincorporated as the City of Brigantine City.

This name lasted until April 9, 1914, when it was renamed the City of East Atlantic City. On March 16, 1924, Brigantine was incorporated as a city, replacing East Atlantic City, and incorporating further portions of Galloway Township. The borough was named for the many shipwrecks in the area, including those of brigantines.

People of Significance – Brigantine

Vincent S. Haneman (April 25, 1902 – January 10, 1978) was an associate justice of the New Jersey Supreme Court from 1960 to 1971 during the era known for the Weintraub Court.

Born in Brooklyn, New York, Haneman was raised in East Orange, New Jersey. He was granted a law degree from Syracuse University College of Law in 1923. His start in public service came in 1926 when he was elected to the Board of Education of the Brigantine Public Schools and was named City Solicitor.

Haneman was a member of the Republican Party. He was Mayor of Brigantine, New Jersey from 1934 to 1942. In 1937, he became assemblyman from Atlantic County in the New Jersey General Assembly and served for seven years. He was the counsel for the New Jersey Racing Commission from 1940 to 1944.

In 1944, Governor of New Jersey Walter E. Edge appointed Haneman to serve on the Court of Common Pleas. He was appointed to the New Jersey Superior Court in 1947. He served as a New Jersey Supreme Court justice from 1960 to 1971 during the era known for the Weintraub Court.

Haneman resided in Brigantine. He died on January 10, 1978, of a heart attack while traveling to his winter home in Naples, Florida.

An American Inns of Court is named in his honor. The Atlantic County, New Jersey Bar Association sponsors the Vincent S. Haneman-Joseph B. Perskie Scholarship. New Jersey Route 87 includes the Justice Vincent S. Haneman Memorial Bridge which crosses the Absecon Channel between Atlantic City and Brigantine.

Harry M. Olivieri (May 25, 1916 – July 22, 2006) was an American restaurateur of Italian descent. He is credited, along with his brother, Pat Olivieri, as the co-creator of the cheesesteak in 1933. The brothers opened Pat's King of Steaks in 1940, one of the best known purveyors of steak sandwiches in Philadelphia.

In the last few years of his life, he lived with his daughter in Brigantine, New Jersey. He died of heart failure on July 22, 2006, in Pomona, New Jersey, at the age of 90.

Ray L. Birdwhistell (September 29, 1918 – October 19, 1994) was an American anthropologist who founded kinesics as a field of inquiry and research. Birdwhistell coined the term kinesics, meaning "facial expression, gestures, posture and gait, and visible arm and body movements." He was born in Brigantine.

Do You Know – Brigantine?

Brigantine has been called **"the best beach on the New Jersey shore"** because of its clean sand, fresh ocean air, and beautiful summer weather.

Brigantine points of interest include **Brigantine Lighthouse and The Brigantine Hotel.**

Brigantine Castle was once a **popular funhouse and haunted house** attraction by the beach in Brigantine. Constructed in 1976, it drew millions of visitors annually until it was damaged in a 1982 storm.

Flanders Hotel in Ocean City, in 1978

All About Ocean City

Ocean City is a city in Cape May County. It is the principal city of the Ocean City metropolitan statistical area, which encompasses all of Cape May County and is part of the Philadelphia-Wilmington-Camden, PA-NJ-DE-MD combined statistical area. It is part of the South Jersey region of the state.

As of the 2010 U.S. census, the city's population was 11,229, a decrease of 472 from the 2010 census count of 11,701, which reflected a decline of 3,677 (−23.9%) from the 15,378 counted in the 2000 census. In summer months, with an influx of tourists and second homeowners, there are estimated to be 115,000 to 130,000 within the city's borders.

Ocean City originated as a borough by an act of the New Jersey Legislature on May 3, 1884, from portions of Upper Township, based on results from a referendum on April 30, 1884, and was reincorporated as a borough on March 31, 1890. Ocean City was incorporated as a city, its current government form, on March 25, 1897. The city is named for its location on the Atlantic Ocean.

Known as a family-oriented seaside resort, Ocean City has not allowed the sale of alcoholic beverages within its limits since its founding in 1879, offering miles of guarded beaches, boardwalk that stretches for 2.5 miles (4.0 km), and a downtown shopping and dining district.

People of Significance – Ocean City

Andrew Cottrell Boswell (September 6, 1873 – February 3, 1936) was a Major League Baseball pitcher. After playing at the University of Pennsylvania he played for the Washington Senators and New York Giants of the National League during the 1895 season. He finished his career in the Western League in 1896. Boswell left baseball and became an attorney, residing in Ocean City.

Preston Stratton Foster (August 24, 1900 – July 14, 1970), was an American actor of stage, film, radio, and television, whose career spanned four decades. He also had a career as a vocalist.

Born in Ocean City in 1900, Foster was the eldest of three children of New Jersey natives Sallie R. (née Stratton) and Walter Foster. Preston had two sisters, Mabel and Anna; and according to federal census records, his family still lived in Ocean City in Cape May County at least as late as 1910.

Preston Foster has a star on the Hollywood Walk of Fame at 6801 Hollywood Blvd.

Keith Andes (born John Charles Andes, July 12, 1920 – November 11, 2005) was an American film, radio, musical theater, stage, and television actor. He was born in Ocean City.

Do You Know – Ocean City?

Known as a **family-oriented** seaside resort, Ocean City has not allowed the sale of alcoholic beverages within its limits since its founding in 1879.

In 1881, the **first school** on the island opened.

In 1965, the **Wonderland Amusement Park** opened on the boardwalk at 6th Street, which is now known as **Gillian's Wonderland Pier.**

The **Ocean City Music Pier** opened in 1929, and is still in full swing, as home to notable comedians and performers, as well as musical productions.

The **Stainton Wildlife Refuge** is an incredible place to go for bird watchers.

All About Margate City

Margate City is a city in Atlantic County. As of the 2020 U.S. census, Margate City's population was 5,317, a reduction of 1,037 over the previous decade. As of the 2010 U.S. census, the city's population was 6,354, reflecting a decline of 1,839 (−22.4%) from the 8,193 counted in the 2000 census, which had in turn declined by 238 (−2.8%) from the 8,431 counted in the 1990 census.

Margate City was originally incorporated as the borough of South Atlantic City by an act of the New Jersey Legislature on September 7, 1885, from portions of Egg Harbor Township, based on the results of a referendum held on August 1, 1885. South Atlantic City was reincorporated as a city on April 23, 1897, and then reincorporated with the name Margate City on April 20, 1909. The city was named for Margate in Kent, England.

The city is located on Absecon Island, which stretches for 8.1 miles (13.0 km) and is also home of Atlantic City and Ventnor City to the northeast, and Longport on the southwest. The city stretches about eight blocks from the Atlantic Ocean to the bay at most points in town. Margate is a popular Jersey Shore destination, especially during the summer, and is the home of Lucy the Elephant, a 65-foot (20 m) wooden elephant, and of Marven Gardens, of Monopoly board game fame.

People of Significance – Margate

Walter Sooy Jeffries (October 16, 1893, Atlantic City – October 11, 1954, Margate City) was an American Republican Party politician who represented New Jersey's 2nd congressional district in the United States House of Representatives from 1939-1941.

He was elected as mayor of Margate City, New Jersey from 1931–1935 and served as sheriff of Atlantic County, New Jersey from 1935-1938. He became engaged in the hotel business at Atlantic City in 1938.

Jeffries was elected as a Republican to the Seventy-sixth Congress, serving in office from January 3, 1939 – January 3, 1941, and was an unsuccessful candidate for reelection in 1940 to the Seventy-seventh Congress. After his term in Congress, he was treasurer of Atlantic County from 1941-1944. Jeffries died in Margate City on October 11, 1954 and was interred in Laurel Memorial Cemetery in Egg Harbor Township, New Jersey.

Louis Herman "Red" Klotz (October 21, 1920 – July 12, 2014) was an American professional basketball player. He was a National Basketball Association (NBA) point guard with the original Baltimore Bullets, and he was best known for forming the teams that play against and tour with the Harlem Globetrotters: the Washington Generals and the New York Nationals. He was the oldest-living NBA champion. He died at age 93 in Margate City where he had long kept his office.

Thomas Charles McGrath Jr. (April 22, 1927, Philadelphia, Pennsylvania – January 15, 1994, Delray Beach, Florida) was an American Democratic Party politician who represented New Jersey's 2nd congressional district in the United States House of Representatives from 1965-1967. McGrath was a resident of Margate City, New Jersey and Juno Beach, Florida, until his death in Delray Beach, Florida, on January 15, 1994.

Do You Know – Margate?

Unlike other seashore towns, Margate has no hotels. Those who choose to visit in the summer are usually residents with second homes.

Margate is the home of **Lucy the Elephant**, the "largest elephant in the world" and is the oldest remaining example of zoomorphic architecture left in the United States. Over 130 years old, she has been painstakingly restored and is toured by thousands of fans each year.

Each summer Margate hosts **"Beachstock."** It's the largest beach party at the Jersey Shore!

All About Sea Isle City

Sea Isle City is a city in Cape May County. It is part of the Ocean City metropolitan statistical area. As of the 2020 United States census, the city's year-round population was 2,104, a decrease of 10 (−0.5%) from the 2010 census count of 2,114, which in turn reflected a decline of 721 (−25.4%) from the 2,835 counted in the 2000 census. Visitors raise the population to as much as 40,000 during the peak summer season from Memorial Day to Labor Day. Sea Isle City is located on Ludlam Island, which also contains the Strathmere section of Upper Township.

Sea Isle City was originally incorporated as a borough on May 22, 1882, from portions of Dennis Township, based on the results of a referendum held six days earlier. The borough was reincorporated on March 31, 1890. In March 1907, portions of Dennis Township and Upper Township were annexed to Sea Isle City. In April 1905, portions of Sea Isle City were annexed to Upper Township. On April 30, 1907, the area was reincorporated as the City of Sea Isle City, based on the results of a referendum held on April 20, 1907. The name derives from its location on the Atlantic Ocean.

People of Significance – Sea Isle City

Charles Kline Landis (March 16, 1833 – June 12, 1900) was a property developer in South Jersey, who was the founder and developer of Vineland and Sea Isle City.

Richard Mead Atwater, Sr. (August 10, 1844 – 1922) was a chemist and public official in New Jersey and Pennsylvania involved in early scientific glass-making.

Atwater married Abby Sophia Greene in 1867 in Providence, Rhode Island. Her family had lived in Greenwich since the Rhode Island colony was started by Roger Williams. Atwater and his wife had nine children,

71

and as their family grew, purchased one of the first oceanside lots at Sea Isle City, New Jersey, where in 1881 he constructed the first summer beach house on the island. It was a simple square structure, built among the dunes, with an open cathedral ceiling two stories high, and bedrooms at the corners of both floors. The family vacationed there for four decades. Atwater was involved in many aspects of life in the town, became the Commodore of the Yacht Club for nine years, and was elected as Mayor of Sea Isle City from 1913 to 1917.

Ann J. Chambers Land (March 12, 1932 in Philadelphia, Pennsylvania – March 9, 2010 in Sea Isle City) was a member of the Philadelphia City Council and a member of the Democratic Party.

Land married her husband, John, in 1954. He was a beverage distributor with a business in West Philadelphia. The couple had five children. She died of chronic obstructive pulmonary disease in March 2010 at her home in Sea Isle City.

Do You Know – Sea Isle City?

Sea Isle City was founded in 1882 by **Charles K. Landis**, who was also the founder of Vineland, New Jersey.

The **"Sara the Turtle Festival"** is one of the city's annual festivals, celebrating a fictional turtle named Sara. Aimed towards families with young children, the festival features live animal exhibits and face painting meant to educate children about the local environment.

During the summer, an **outdoor Band Shell** located in the heart of the downtown beachfront district offers free entertainment such as concerts, family dance parties, "Movies Under the Stars," and "Sea Isle City's Got Talent" contests.

All About North Wildwood

North Wildwood is a city located on the Jersey Shore in Cape May County. It is part of the Ocean City metropolitan statistical area. As of the 2020 United States census, the city's population was 3,621, a decrease of 420 (−10.4%) from the 2010 census count of 4,041, which in turn reflected a decline of 894 (−18.1%) from the 4,935 counted in the 2000 census. North Wildwood is home to the Hereford Inlet Lighthouse.

The city's beaches were ranked the fourth-best in New Jersey in the 2008 Top 10 Beaches Contest sponsored by the New Jersey Marine Sciences Consortium. North Wildwood is one of five municipalities in the state that offer free public access to oceanfront beaches monitored by lifeguards, joining Atlantic City, Wildwood, Wildwood Crest and Upper Township's Strathmere section.

People of Significance – North Wildwood

Anthony James Cafiero (February 11, 1900 – September 28, 1982) was a member of the New Jersey Senate from 1949 to 1953.

He was born on February 11, 1900, in Philadelphia, Pennsylvania, the son of a Philadelphia barber. He moved to North Wildwood, in 1921. He was the Cape May County prosecutor from 1944 to 1946, and was a county judge in Cape May County from 1946 to 1948.

He was a member of the New Jersey Senate, representing Cape May County as a Republican, from 1948 to 1954. He served in the New Jersey Superior Court from 1954 until retiring in 1970. He died on September 28, 1982, in Middle Township, New Jersey.

Thomas Francis "Cozy" Morley (c. 1926 – August 23, 2013) was an American singer-songwriter, entertainer, comedian and club owner, best known for his rendition of "On the Way to Cape May," which became his signature song.

The nickname "Cozy" came because he looked like he could be the younger brother of an entertainer named Cozy Dolan. He was described by The New York Times as having been a "South Jersey Shore institution" starting from the time when he was first discovered in 1949 and brought to the attention of Ed Suez, who owned a club in North Wildwood, New Jersey and hired him as an opening act; building on his success as a performer, Morley bought the club from Suez in 1958 for $10,000. Though he didn't create the song, Morley helped popularize the song "On the Way to Cape May," a song that became Morely's signature song, chronicling the places encountered along the route.

A statue of Morley stands at the former site of Club Avalon in North Wildwood, which he owned and operated until 1989, when the city condemned the building. He attracted crowds as large as 1,200 to his club. The city's mayor called him "Mr. North Wildwood." After his club closed, Morley performed frequently in Atlantic City.

In the late 1990s, Morley competed in an annual Tramcar Race as a fundraiser on the Wildwood/North Wildwood boardwalk against entertainer Al Alberts.

A longtime resident of Haddon Township, New Jersey, Morley also owned homes in North Wildwood and in Fort Lauderdale, Florida. Morley died on August 23, 2013, at a hospital in Camden. The cause of death was complications related to diabetes.

Morley was inducted into the Broadcast Pioneers of Philadelphia Hall of Fame in 2015.

James S. Cafiero (born September 21, 1928) is an American Republican Party politician, who served in the New Jersey General Assembly from 1968 to 1972 and in the New Jersey Senate from 1972 to 1982 and from 1990 to 2004, where he represented the 1st legislative district. He was born in North Wildwood.

Do You Know – North Wildwood?

In the early 1600s, the **Lenni Lenape Indians** visited North Wildwood each summer to fish, relax and cool off on these beaches.

The Wildwoods' **beaches stretch for five miles** across the shores of North Wildwood, Wildwood, and Wildwood Crest. They are wide, clean, and free!

Cool Scoops Ice Cream in North Wildwood has hosted music legends like Bobby Rydell, Chubby Checker, Mary Wilson of the Supremes, and Buddy Holly's original Crickets.

On April 14, 1997, The Space Shuttle Columbia was launched from the Kennedy Space Center Florida. Astronaut Gregory Linteris, a New Jersey native, took Eastern White Pine seedlings with him on the flight. NASA gave those seeds to the New Jersey Forestry Service which grew only thirty-five trees. The seeds germinated in seven days, about one half of the germination time. They were dedicated to the memory of the seven-crew member of the crew that perished in the Columbia Space Shuttle in 2003.

A tree stands today in Cape May that from those space shuttle seeds. Do you know where? Answer on page 76.

All About Wildwood

Wildwood is a city in Cape May County. It is part of the Ocean City metropolitan statistical area and a popular Jersey Shore summer resort destination. As of the 2020 United States census, the city's year-round population was 5,157, a decrease of 168 (−3.2%) from the 2010 census count of 5,325, which in turn reflected a decline of 111 (−2.0%) from the 5,436 counted in the 2000 census. With visitors, the population can swell to 250,000 during the summer. Wildwood was the first city in New Jersey to have a female mayor, Doris W. Bradway, who was ousted in a 1938 recall election.

The Wildwoods is used as a collective term to describe four communities on the island with the name Wildwood attached to them: North Wildwood, West Wildwood, Wildwood, and Wildwood Crest. Also part of The Wildwoods are Diamond Beach and a portion of Lower Township on the island. The city, and the surrounding communities that share the name, derives its name from the wildflowers found in the area. Wildwood is part of the South Jersey region of the state.

People of Significance – Wildwood

Jacob Thompson Baker (April 13, 1847 – December 7, 1919) was an American Democratic Party politician from New Jersey who represented New Jersey's 2nd congressional district for one term from 1913 to 1915.

Answer from page 75: Astronaut Gregory Linteris, a New Jersey native, took Eastern White Pine seeds with him on that flight. NASA gave those seeds to the New Jersey Forestry Service. This tree is located at Colonial House Museum, Cape May.

He was chairman of the Democratic State convention in 1905. Baker moved to New Jersey and was one of the founders of Wildwood and the borough of Wildwood Crest. He was the first Mayor of Wildwood, New Jersey in 1911 and 1912, and was a delegate to the 1912 Democratic National Convention.

Baker was elected as a Democrat to the Sixty-third Congress, serving in office from March 4, 1913, to March 3, 1915, but was an unsuccessful candidate for reelection in 1914 to the Sixty-fourth Congress.

After leaving Congress, he resumed real estate activities in Wildwood.

Joy Bright Hancock (4 May 1898 – 20 August 1986), a veteran of both the First and Second World Wars, was one of the first women officers of the United States Navy. She was born in Wildwood on 4 May 1898. During World War I, after attending business school in Philadelphia, Pennsylvania, she enlisted in the Navy as a Yeoman (F), serving at Camden, New Jersey and at Naval Air Station Wildwood.

Edwin Corle (May 7, 1906 – June 11, 1956) was an American writer. He was born in Wildwood and educated at the University of California, Berkeley, where he received his A.B. in 1928. For the next two years he was a graduate student at Yale University. His writing is noted for realistic portrayals of American Indian life in the early 20th century.

Do You Know – Wildwood?

"Rock Around the Clock," often credited as the first rock and roll record, was first performed on Memorial Day weekend in 1954 at the **HofBrau Hotel in Wildwood by Bill Haley & His Comets**. The song's status as one of the first rock and roll hits has given rise to the city's claim as "the birthplace of rock and roll."

Chubby Checker introduced his version of "The Twist" at the Rainbow Club in Wildwood.

On occasion, **American Bandstand** broadcast from the **Wildwood's Starlight Ballroom**.

Bobby Rydell's major hit, "Wildwood Days" in 1963, is about Wildwood.

Murals in the Wildwood community honor Checker, Bill Haley; and Bobby Rydell.

Wildwood has the **highest concentration of 1950s-style motels** in the world. These motels are a beloved landmark in the community and have been cherished by both locals and visitors alike for decades.

More **than 200 motels were built during the Doo-Wop** era of the 1950s and 1960s. The term "doo-wop" was coined by Cape May's Mid-Atlantic Center for the Arts in the early 1990s to describe the unique, space-age architectural style, which is also referred to as the "Googie" or "populuxe" style. The motels are unique in appearance, with Vegas-like neon signs and fantastic architecture.

A **Wildwood 1950s Doo-Wop Museum** includes property from de-molished motels such as neon signs and furniture. In June 2006, its Doo-Wop-style motels were placed on the National Trust for Historic Preser-vation's annual Eleven Most Endangered List, described as "irreplaceable icons of popular culture."

The boardwalk features a trolley called the "**Tramcar," which runs from end to end.**

Boardwalk Chapel is a summertime Christian Gospel outreach on the boardwalk, sandwiched between a pizzeria and a gift shop. Visitors to the boardwalk are invited to attend any of its seventy-seven consecu-tive evening services held during June, July, and August.

A portion of the **rock band Kiss's 1975 album Alive!** was recorded from a July 23, 1975 concert at the old Wildwoods Convention Center.

Wildwood has one of the **longest bike paths** on the East Coast - stretching 12 miles from the boardwalk to North Wildwood sea wall.

All About Wildwood Crest

Wildwood Crest is a borough in Cape May County. It is part of the Ocean City metropolitan statistical area in the South Jersey region of the state. As of the 2020 United States census, the borough's population was 3,101, a decrease of 169 (−5.2%) from the 2010 census count of 3,270, which in turn reflected a decline of 710 (−17.8%) from the 3,980 counted in the 2000 census.

Wildwood Crest was incorporated as a borough by an act of the New Jersey Legislature on April 6, 1910, from portions of Lower Township. The area of the borough was first developed by Philip Baker in the 1910s as a southern extension to the resort of Wildwood. The borough's name comes from Wildwood, which in turn was named for the area's wild flowers.

It is a dry town, where alcohol cannot be sold, affirmed by the results of a referendum held in 1940. Wildwood Crest joins Cape May Point and Ocean City among municipalities in Cape May restricting the sale of alcohol. Adjoining Wildwood allows the sale of alcohol, including at bars on its boardwalk.

The borough was ranked the second-best beach in New Jersey in the 2008 "Top 10 Beaches Contest" sponsored by the New Jersey Marine Sciences Consortium. Wildwood Crest is one of five municipalities in the state that offer free public access to oceanfront beaches monitored by lifeguards, joining Atlantic City, North Wildwood, Wildwood and Upper Township's Strathmere section.

People of Significance – Wildwood Crest

Aliki Liacouras Brandenberg or pen name Aliki (born September 3, 1929) is an American author and illustrator of books for children. She was born in Wildwood Crest.

She has written and illustrated many books, and she has also illustrated books for other authors, including her husband Franz Brandenberg. Brandenberg's career as an author and illustrator led her to explore many subjects of historic and scientific interest. Her nonfiction books, either written by herself or by others, touch upon matters as varied as dinosaurs, mammoths, book manufacturing, Shakespeare, evolution, and growing up. Aliki's fictional works explore such themes as family and friendship. Brandenberg's Greek heritage is also a recurring theme in her works, both fiction and nonfiction.

Kenneth Algernon Black Jr. (December 23, 1932 – January 29, 2019) was an American Republican Party politician who served in the New Jersey General Assembly from District 3A from 1968 to 1974.

A resident of Wildwood Crest since1984, he died there on January 29, 2019, at age 86.

Bernard Marcel Parent (born April 3, 1945) is a Canadian former professional ice hockey goaltender who played 13 National Hockey League (NHL) seasons with the Philadelphia Flyers, Boston Bruins, and Toronto Maple Leafs, and also spent one season in the World Hockey Association (WHA) with the Philadelphia Blazers. Parent is widely acknowledged as one of the greatest goaltenders of all time.

Parent has been a resident of Cherry Hill, New Jersey and had a shore house in Wildwood Crest, where he lived most of the years. For seven months of every year, he lives on his 45-foot yacht named The French Connection.

Do You Know – Wildwood Crest?

In Wildwood Crest, several **"Doo Wop" motels**, such as the Caribbean Motel, are registered on the National Register of Historic Places. In recent years, historic "Doo Wop" motels have been demolished to make way for the construction of condominiums, leading to organized efforts to preserve the remaining examples.

Part of the Wildwood Crest borough's **beachfront has been closed** off for the protection of native birds such as the piping plover. These small birds have this area all to themselves so that their eggs may be protected from beachgoers.

Wildwood Crest is a dry town which joins Cape May Point and Ocean City among municipalities in Cape May restricting the sale of alcohol.

Q: Where is this mansion located?
Answer on page 82

All About Avalon

Avalon is a borough in Cape May County. It is located on Seven Mile Island, neighbors Stone Harbor and is situated between Ocean City, Wildwood, and Cape May. As of the 2020 U.S. census, the full-time borough population was 1,243, a decline of 91 from the 2010 census enumeration of 1,334, which in turn declined by 809 (−37.8%) from the 2,143 counted in the 2000 census. The borough's population swells during the summer months.

Geographically part of the South Jersey region, the community is one of the most affluent communities along the Jersey Shore and is home to some of the most expensive real estate on the East Coast.

In 2007, Forbes listed Avalon as the 65th most expensive ZIP Code in the United States. Washingtonian even "named Avalon the 'chicest beach' in the mid-Atlantic, the place to see women in diamonds and designer swimwear." A small portion of Avalon is not on Seven Mile Island. The borough is part of the Ocean City Metropolitan Statistical Area.

Avalon is known as a South Jersey seashore resort and has the motto "Cooler by a Mile" since it juts out into the Atlantic Ocean about a mile farther than other barrier islands. Alternatively, the motto is because Avalon, at four miles long, is one mile longer than its neighboring town on the southern end of Seven Mile Island, Stone Harbor. It was ranked the seventh-best beach in New Jersey in the 2008 Top 10 Beaches Contest sponsored by the New Jersey Marine Sciences Consortium.

Avalon has a half-mile boardwalk for scenic strolls and bike riding, plus public tennis courts, basketball courts, a skate park, and large playgrounds to enjoy.

Answer from page 81: Cape May

People of Significance – Avalon

Edward Leo Peter McMahon Jr. (March 6, 1923 – June 23, 2009) was an American announcer, game show host, comedian, actor, singer, and combat aviator. McMahon and Johnny Carson began their association in their first TV series, the ABC game show Who Do You Trust? running from 1957 to 1962. McMahon then made his famous thirty-year mark as Carson's sidekick, announcer and second banana on NBC's The Tonight Show Starring Johnny Carson from 1962 to 1992.

McMahon also hosted the original Star Search from 1983 to 1995, co-hosted TV's Bloopers & Practical Jokes with Dick Clark from 1982 to 1998, presented sweepstakes for American Family Publishers, annually co-hosted the Jerry Lewis MDA Telethon from 1973 to 2008 and anchored the team of NBC personalities covering the Macy's Thanksgiving Day Parade during the 1970s and '80s.

McMahon appeared in several films, including The Incident, Fun with Dick and Jane, Full Moon High and Butterfly, as well as briefly in the film version of the TV sitcom Bewitched and also performed in numerous television commercials. According to Entertainment Weekly, McMahon is considered one of the greatest "sidekicks." McMahon was a longtime summer resident of Avalon.

Michael W. Rice (born December 9, 1943), son of Francis Xavier Rice and Arlene (Utz) Rice of Hanover, Pennsylvania, is a 3rd generation American businessman serving as Director, Chairman Emeritus, and Special Advisor to Utz of Utz Quality Foods, Inc. Rice's current house in Avalon, New Jersey covering 20,000 square feet (1,900 m) was initially rejected by state and municipal authorities; it was ultimately agreed to limit the house to 40 rooms.

Luigi "Geno" Auriemma (born March 23, 1954) is an Italian-born American college basketball coach and, since 1985, the head coach of the University of Connecticut Huskies women's basketball team. Auriemma was inducted into the Naismith Memorial Basketball Hall of Fame and the Women's Basketball Hall of Fame in 2006. For many years, Auriemma and his wife, Kathy, maintained a home in Avalon, to be near their parents in the Philadelphia area.

83

Do You Know – Avalon?

The Avalon area was purchased by **Aaron Leaming** in December 1722 for seventy-nine pounds.

The Avalon community is one of the most affluent communities along the Jersey Shore and is home to some of the most expensive real estate on the East Coast. The Washingtonian, a monthly magazine distributed in Washington, D.C. named Avalon the "chicest beach" in the mid-Atlantic, the place to see women in diamonds and designer swimwear.

Kohler's Bakery, known for serving baked items made from scratch, has been a part *of the community of Avalon since 1949.*

Question: What is this building?
Answer on page 85

All About Cape May

Cape May is a city located at the southern tip of Cape May Peninsula in Cape May County. Located where the Delaware Bay meets the Atlantic Ocean, it is one of the country's oldest vacation resort destinations, and part of the Ocean City metropolitan statistical area.

As of the 2020 United States census, the city's year-round population was 2,768, a decrease of 839 (−23.3%) from the 2010 census count of 3,607, which in turn reflected a decline of 427 (−10.6%) from the 4,034 counted in the 2000 census. In the summer, Cape May's population is expanded by as many as 40,000 to 50,000 visitors. The entire city of Cape May is designated the Cape May Historic District, a National Historic Landmark due to its concentration of Victorian architecture.

People of Significance – Cape May

Thomas Hurst Hughes (January 10, 1769 – November 10, 1839) was a U.S. Representative from New Jersey.

Born in the Cold Spring section of Lower Township, New Jersey, on January 10, 1769; he attended the public schools. He moved to Cape May City in 1800 and engaged in the mercantile business; in 1816 he built Congress Hall, which he managed for many years; he also served as sheriff of Cape May County from 1801 to 1804. Hughes was a member of the New Jersey General Assembly from 1805 to 1807, in 1809, 1812, and 1813; and a member of the New Jersey Legislative Council (now the New Jersey Senate) from 1819 to 1823 and in 1824 and 1825.

Answer from page 84: A former lighthouse in Avalon

Jarena Lee (February 11, 1783 – February 3, 1864) was the first woman preacher in the African Methodist Episcopal Church (AME). Born into a free Black family, in New Jersey, Lee asked the founder of the AME church, Richard Allen, to be a preacher.

Although Allen initially refused, after hearing her preach in 1819, Allen approved her preaching ministry. A leader in the Wesleyan-Holiness movement, Lee preached the doctrine of entire sanctification as an itinerant pastor throughout the pulpits of the African Methodist Episcopal denomination. In 1836, Lee became the first African American woman to publish her autobiography. Jarena Lee was born on February 11, 1783, in Cape May.

Witmer Stone (September 22, 1866 – May 24, 1939) was an American ornithologist, botanist, and mammalogist, and was considered one of the last of the "great naturalists."

For all of his work as one of the preeminent ornithologists of his day, Stone's most enduring popular legacy is undoubtedly his charming Bird Studies at Old Cape May (BSOCM), originally published by the Delaware Valley Ornithological Club (DVOC) in 1937. This was an ornithological history of the New Jersey coast, with an emphasis on Cape May County, particularly the coastal areas.

The bulk of the work consists of species accounts of all the birds that had been found in Cape May County at the time of the writing, with their historical occurrence in the state and notes on seasonality, habits, behavior, etc. gleaned from Stone's own notes and the records of fellow DVOC members. Stone dedicated Bird Studies at Old Cape May to his wife. Stone first visited Cape May in August 1890, and spent most of July–August 1891 there.

He made frequent trips there over the years and became an annual summer resident starting in 1916 and continuing until at least 1937. The largest photograph of Stone hangs in the Cape May Bird Observatory's Center for Research and Education in Goshen, New Jersey.

Do You Know – Cape May?

Cape May was **founded in 1620** by Captain Cornelius Jacobsen Mey, a Dutch navigator.

Cape May is the **oldest seaside resort in America** and is also known as the "Queen of the Seaside Resorts."

Cape May is home to the **largest collection of Victorian homes** in America, many of which are open to the public for tours.

The Cape May **Lighthouse**, built in 1859, is the third oldest operating lighthouse in the country.

The Cape May **Point State Park** offers visitors a chance to see a wide variety of migratory birds and other wildlife.

Cape May is home to the **Mid-Atlantic Center for the Arts & Humanities**, which offers a wide range of tours, events, and programs that focus on the city's history and culture.

Cape May is also a **popular spot for fishing** and boating. Popular species include flounder, striped bass, and bluefish.

Cape May is home to the **Naval Air Station Wildwood Aviation** Museum, which features exhibits on the military history of the area.

Cape May is home to the **Cape May Music Festival**, an annual event featuring a wide range of classical and jazz performances.

The Victorian era brought about **a new wave of development to** Cape May with many grand hotels being built along its coastline. During this time period, some of America's wealthiest families began vacationing at these resorts.

In 1816, Congress passed legislation that allowed for the construction of lighthouses along the coast of New Jersey to help guide ships safely into port. **The first lighthouse built in Cape May** was completed in 1823 and there have been two others built on the same location. The lighthouse still stands today as one of the most iconic landmarks on the island.

Treasures of the Jersey Shore

Beaches

New Jersey has forty-four beaches which span the coast from Sandy Hook in the north, to Cape May at the southern tip. These go-to summer destinations are not only embraced by locals, but tourists as well.

Boardwalks

New Jersey is the location of most of the boardwalks in the United States. New Jersey has eighteen boardwalks. With arcades, amusement parks, and water parks boasting hundreds of rides and attractions,

New Jersey's top boardwalks to explore are: Point Pleasant Beach, Seaside Heights, Atlantic City, Ocean City, and Wildwood.

Casinos

Atlantic City is filled with glitzy high-rise hotels and nightclubs. In addition to gambling at slot machines and table games, the casinos offer spa treatments, performances by famous comedy and music acts, and high-end shopping.

As of 2023, New Jersey has nine casinos, all in Atlantic City. They are regulated by the New Jersey Casino Control Commission and New Jersey Division of Gaming Enforcement.

The Food Scene

When you travel to the Jersey Shore you will find every type of cuisine. There are some great restaurants where one can sit waterside and enjoy the gorgeous view as they enjoy their meal.

Of course, when you are on the boardwalk, there is plenty of food to choose from: hot dogs, steak sandwiches, pizza, and salt-water taffy. Or drink some of the fresh squeezed lemonade. One big thing about visiting the Jersey Shore and its many boardwalks, promenades and snack bars is that anything can be fried, and it will be delicious. Oreos, candy bars, twinkies and those amazing intertangled webs of dough we know as funnel cakes can all be enjoyed down the shore.

The Music Scene

The Jersey shore is the place to go for musical action. Asbury Park is known for the Stone Pony and Asbury Lanes, but you can also hear live music on the boardwalk, as well as inside venues, in Atlantic City on any given summer night.

Ocean City has a music pier where you can go to see classic rock, as well as folk. And Wildwood has music at their Oceanfront Arena as well as the Wildwoods Convention Center.

There are also plenty of smaller venues, like bars and restaurants, that have live music indoors or on their seaside patios.

Island Beach State Park

Most visitors come to Island Beach State Park for the white sand beach, the ocean waters, and natural backdrop, in contrast to the developed and boardwalk-lined beaches to the north and south. Island Beach State Park encompasses many miles of beach; the northernmost have lifeguards. People can swim, surf, fish, and kayak in the park. The park also allows dune buggy access in the southern portion of the park. There is also a boardwalk extending from Barnegat Bay to the main road allowing boaters access to the beach. On the bayside of Island Beach State Park is an area called Tices Shoal, where boaters gather and anchor.

Light Houses

Jersey Shore lighthouses are another tourist attraction. Along the Jersey shore stand ten, original, noble lighthouses, which have helped sailors navigate safely since as far back as the 1700s.

The four working lighthouses on the New Jersey shore are the Absecon Lighthouse in Atlantic City, Barnegat Lighthouse in Barnegat

Maryanne Christiano-Mistretta

Light, Cape May Lighthouse in Cape May, and Hereford Inlet Lighthouse in North Wildwood. These lighthouses have been guiding ships since the 1800s and are still standing today.

Visiting these lighthouses is a great way to experience a piece of New Jersey history while also enjoying some stunning views of the ocean. The Absecon Lighthouse is the tallest lighthouse in New Jersey at 171 feet tall and offers breathtaking views from its top platform. The Barnegat Lighthouse is one of the most iconic lighthouses on the east coast and has been featured in many movies and television shows. The Cape May Lighthouse has been standing since 1859 and provides visitors with a unique look into maritime history. Finally, the Hereford Inlet Lighthouse is located near beautiful beaches and offers visitors an up-close look at its historic architecture.

The Steel Pier

The Steel Pier is a 1,000-foot-long (300 m) amusement park built on a pier of the boardwalk in Atlantic City, New Jersey, across from the Hard Rock Hotel & Casino Atlantic City (formerly the Trump Taj Mahal). Begun in 1898, it was one of the most popular venues in the United States for the first seven decades of the twentieth century, featuring concerts, exhibits, and an amusement park. It billed itself as the Showplace of the Nation and at its peak measured 2,298 feet (700 m). The Steel Pier continues to operate as an amusement pier and is one of the most successful family-oriented attractions in the city.

The Edwin B. Forsythe National Wildlife Refuge

The Edwin B. Forsythe National Wildlife Refuge is a United States National Wildlife Refuge located in southern New Jersey along the Atlantic coast north of Atlantic City, in Atlantic and Ocean counties. It's known for scenic trails going through coastal wetlands, freshwater ponds, and woodlands. It's a great location for bird watching, hiking, taking photographs, and witnessing gorgeous views of the Atlantic City skyline.

Hidden Beaches Along the Jersey Shore

Holgate Beach

Holgate is a seashore town at the southernmost end of Long Beach Island. Holgate is most popular for fishing at the marina. Being alone with just the ocean and sand dunes, it's truly a nature lover's paradise. Best of all a stunning view of the Atlantic City skyline, especially at sunset.

Higbee Beach

Higbee Beach is located at the tip of Cape May Island. It's known for bird watching, picnics, calm waters, gorgeous sunsets, and even nude sunbathing. Dogs are welcome on the beach too. The best part of this hidden gem is, it's a free beach.

Pearl Beach

Pearl Beach is another quieter, lesser crowded treasure located at the southernmost tip of Cape May. As you lay out on the white sand, you're sure to see lots of birds, butterflies, dragonflies, seagulls, as well as dolphins.

Strathmere Beach

Strathmere Beach is not even two miles long. It's a free beach where you can raft, surf, and fish. A lifeguard is on duty during the season and beach patrol utilizes the flag warning system to let swimmers know the rip tide conditions.

Sunset Beach

Sunset Beach is a beach located on the Cape May Peninsula, in Lower Township, near Cape May Point, along the Delaware Bay. It is a local tourist attraction due in part to its proximity to the SS Atlantus, also known as the Concrete Ship, and the Cape May Lighthouse.

Quotes About the Jersey Shore

Actor Danny DeVito has said that he loves spending time at the Jersey Shore, particularly in Wildwood. He's quoted as saying "I love Wildwood…It's like a little piece of heaven on earth."

Actress and singer Mandy Moore also loves visiting the Jersey Shore. She's said that she loves going to Avalon and Stone Harbor because they are "so peaceful and beautiful."

Question: What is the name of this beach?
Answer on page 93

The Best Walking Trails on the Jersey Shore

The Jersey Shore is home to some of the most beautiful hiking trails in the country. From sandy beaches to lush forests, there is something for everyone. One of the best trails on the Jersey Shore is **Stone Cutter Trail**. This 4.4-mile loop trail offers views of the Atlantic Ocean and passes through a variety of habitats including wetlands, meadows, and forests. Along the way, hikers can spot various wildlife such as birds and deer and enjoy scenic overlooks with breathtaking views of the shoreline.

The 4.5-mile **Bob Webber Trail** takes hikers through marshlands, woodlands, and open fields. Along this trail, hikers can spot various wildlife such as turtles and frogs while taking in beautiful views of Barnegat Bay and its surrounding islands.

The Jersey Shore to Pine Creek via Pine Creek Rail Trail is a great option for hikers looking for an adventure on the shoreline. This 4.5-mile out-and-back trail takes hikers through a variety of habitats including wetlands, meadows, and forests while offering stunning views of Pine Creek Valley along with its many creeks and streams that flow into it from nearby mountainsides.

Mid-State Trail: Little Gap to Wind Gap Loop is a more challenging trail, offering 8 miles of rugged terrain with elevation changes and spectacular views of the countryside from atop rocky ridges and cliffsides overlooking valleys below and several waterfalls.

If you're looking for something more relaxing head to **Gateway National Recreation Area Loop** for 5 miles of easy terrain perfect for leisurely strolls or birdwatching, with stunning views of Sandy Hook Bay and its surrounding islands.

Answer from page 92: Wildwood Beach

Handicap Accessible Walking Trails

For those with mobility issues, the **Henry Hudson Trail/Popamora Point** offers **handicap accessible trails** with breathtaking ocean views. The 8-mile loop runs along the Atlantic Highlands and is wheelchair friendly, featuring wide paths and gradual inclines. **Cattus Island County Park** is a handicap accessible trail, featuring over 800 acres of land and 20 miles of trails, including wide pathways perfect for wheelchairs or other mobility devices. The park features boardwalks perfect for bird watching or taking in the sights of the surrounding area.

The Best Birding Trails on the Jersey Shore

AllTrails.com is a great place to find the best birding trails, from easy hikes to more challenging treks, all with beautiful scenery and plenty of birds. The **NJ Birding & Wildlife Trails** program provides information about some of the best birding spots, including Island Beach State Park and Gateway National Recreation Area (Sandy Hook).

Check out **NJ Spots' list of Best New Jersey Birding Spots** or browse through **TrailLink's Top Birding Trails & Maps in New Jersey** for detailed maps and descriptions. You can find out about upcoming bird walks at places like **Frank Chapman Birding Trail (Teaneck)** or **Richard W. DeKorte Park** by reading "An At-a-Glance Guide to 2022 Bird Walks in NJ" from *NJ Monthly Magazine*.

Local wildlife refuges like **North Brigantine Natural Area** and **Natural Lands' Glades Wildlife Refuge**, and **Port Republic Wildlife Management Area** offer truly unique bird watching experiences.

The Best Children Friendly Walking Trails

From the Gateway National Recreation Area Loop to the Henry Hudson Trail, there are plenty of child-friendly trails that offer stunning views and plenty of fun. The **Edgar Felix Memorial Bikeway** is a great option for families with young children. This paved trail runs along the Manasquan River and offers beautiful views of the water and opportunities to spot wildlife. The **Cape May Point Trail** offers historical sites such as lighthouses, old military fortifications, and more.

The New Jersey Coastal Heritage Trail

The New Jersey Coastal Heritage Trail is not really a trail, it is a route designed to be leisurely seen by auto for the benefit of the public to provide education, understanding, and enjoyment of natural, maritime, and cultural sites of the coastal area of New Jersey.

The concept is to join together the Jersey shore areas into five regions with three major themes; Coastal Habitat, Maritime Heritage, and Wildlife Migration.

The trail hugs the coastline of New Jersey and runs 300 miles, being divided into regions from Sandy Hook Region along New York Harbor, south to Barnegat Bay Region, the Absecon Cape May Region, and the Delsea Region along Delaware Bay. You will be able to meander along the area east of the Garden State Parkway from the Raritan Bay south to the area north and west of Cape May and south of Route 49 to the vicinity of Deepwater.

The trail includes many New Jersey state parks and facilities with all of the Trail's destinations loosely owned and operated by other agencies and organizations.

Since September 30, 2011, as a result of a sunset clause, the National Park Service is no longer the legislative authority to be involved in the management of the Trail. At this time there is no single authority responsible for the management of the trail, although there are legislative efforts to reinstate the NPS as the legislative authority.

Although The New Jersey Coastal Heritage Trail Route is designed for vehicular touring, it connects areas of interest to hikers. In addition to the five themes, The Coastal Heritage Trail is divided into five regions, linked by the common heritage of life on the Jersey Shore and the Raritan and Delaware bays.

The Secrets of the Jersey Shore

The Jersey Shore has long been known as one of America's greatest summer spots, and with good reason. With gorgeous beaches, charming towns, and cities, and plenty of attractions and activities, it's no surprise that so many people flock to this area every year. However, there are some hidden gems in this region that you may not know about – here are a few of the secrets of the Jersey Shore!

First off, if you're looking for a spot away from all the hustle and bustle of typical tourist areas, head to Island Beach State Park. This pristine barrier island is just ten miles south of Seaside Heights and offers miles of untouched beachfront beauty. Camping is available from April through October in over forty rustic sites, or you can stay in one of the two cabins on the island. There's also a sand dune full of paths perfect for bird watching or taking a leisurely stroll along the shoreline.

For those wanting to explore more than just beaches during their stay at the Jersey shore, Spring Lake is an unexpected treat! It's often overlooked since it isn't located near any boardwalk cities, but this delightful town is worth seeking out thanks to its lush parks and tree-lined streets. Spend your days visiting local art galleries or shopping in unique boutiques before ending your day at one of several lovely restaurants tucked throughout town.

If it's an outdoor adventure, you desire while visiting Jersey Shore then head down to Edwin B Forsythe Wildlife Preserve near Atlantic City. Here you can spend time bird watching or take a boat tour around the huge salt marsh area which is home to thousands of different species like egrets, geese, and horseshoe crabs! If kayaking is more your style then head into Barnegat Bay where you can get up close with dolphins as well as many varieties of waterfowl like herons and ibis'.

There are plenty more adventure awaiting those who visit Jersey Shore each year - including lighthouses open for tours, segway tours offering incredible views of the coastline, kayak tours exploring rivers winding through picturesque wetlands - so don't miss out on these more off-the-beaten-path activities when planning your summer getaway!

The Jersey Shore is home to many ocean-related secrets, both hidden and known. From the secret fishing spots only, locals know about to the mysterious shipwrecks scattered along the coast, this stretch of coastline is full of fascinating tales and mysteries.

One of the most well-known secrets of the shore is its history as a hideout for pirates. During the 18th century, many pirates sailed up and down the Atlantic in search of treasure ships, and some even hid out among islands off the New Jersey Coast. The most notorious of them all was "Blackbeard" who made his home in Barnegat Bay near Long Beach Island. It was said he kept his treasures buried along the shore, but no one has ever been able to prove it.

Even today there are still plenty of secrets lurking in and around the waters off New Jersey's coast. Fishermen are kept busy searching for flounder, stripers, bluefish, sea bass and other fish that lurk beneath the waves. But there's more than just fish lurking down below - strange creatures like giant squid have been spotted in deep waters, while unusual artifacts like ancient shipwrecks dot seabed floors.

Despite its reputation as a hotspot for vacationers looking for sun and sand, the Jersey Shore is also teeming with wildlife - from dolphins to sharks to seabirds searching for food or shelter in tide pools or mangrove swamps. Of course, there are also plenty of crabs scurrying across shallow areas in search of their next meal.

The mystery surrounding this area doesn't stop with its marine life though; just offshore from Asbury Park lies an old abandoned military fort dating all the way back to 1798 that once served as a storage facility for secret Confederate weapons during Civil War times! Even today people will take boat trips out far enough into open water to get a glimpse at its remains before making their way back safely to shore.

The secrets beneath these waves don't just stop here either – some believe that numerous sunken treasure ships lie at rest beneath these waters waiting to be discovered by some brave soul willing to explore them! Whether you're looking for lost pirate gold or ancient artifacts from centuries past, you can be sure that if you're willing to venture out far enough you'll find something amazing lurking beneath these waves!

The Jersey Shore is home to many secrets, both hidden and known. From the secret fishing spots only locals know about to the mysterious shipwrecks scattered along the coast, this stretch of coastline is full of fascinating tales and mysteries.

Question: What is the name of this lighthouse?
Answer on page 99

Celebrities/Famous People

The Jersey Shore is very popular, so it is no surprise that it is a home and common vacation spot for many celebrities and famous people. Here are some examples:

Kevin Smith (Born in Red Bank)

Kevin Patrick Smith (born August 2, 1970) is an American filmmaker, actor, comedian, comic book writer, author, YouTuber, and podcaster. He came to prominence with the low-budget comedy buddy film Clerks (1994), which he wrote, directed, co-produced, and acted in as the character Silent Bob of stoner duo Jay and Silent Bob—characters who also appeared in Smith's later films Mallrats (1995), Chasing Amy (1997), Dogma (1999), (2001), Clerks II (2006), Jay and Silent Bob Reboot (2019), and Clerks III (2022). All films are set primarily in his home state of New Jersey. While not strictly sequential, the films have crossover plot elements, character references, and a shared canon known as the "View Askewniverse," named after Smith's production company View Askew Productions, which he co-founded with Scott Mosier.

Smith owns Jay and Silent Bob's Secret Stash in Red Bank, a comic book store which became the setting for the reality television show Comic Book Men (2012–2018). He also hosts the movie-review TV show Spoilers. As a podcaster, Smith cohosts several shows on his SModcast Podcast Network, including SModcast, Fatman Beyond, and the live show Hollywood Babble-On. He is known for participating in long, humorous Q&A sessions that are often filmed for DVD release, beginning with An Evening with Kevin Smith.

Answer from page 98: Barnegat Lighthouse

Bruce Springsteen (Born in Long Branch)

Bruce Frederick Joseph Springsteen (born September 23, 1949) is an American singer, songwriter, and musician. He has released 21 studio albums, most of which feature his backing band, the E Street Band. He is an originator of heartland rock, combining mainstream rock musical styles with narrative songs about working class American life. Nicknamed "The Boss," his career has spanned six decades. Springsteen is known for his poetic, socially conscious lyrics, and energetic stage performances which sometimes last up to four hours.

Among the album era's prominent acts, Springsteen has sold more than 140 million records worldwide and more than 71 million in the United States, making him one of the world's best-selling music artists. He has earned numerous awards for his work, including 20 Grammy Awards, two Golden Globes, an Academy Award, and a Special Tony Award (for Springsteen on Broadway). Springsteen was inducted into both the Songwriters Hall of Fame and the Rock and Roll Hall of Fame in 1999, received the Kennedy Center Honors in 2009, named MusiCares person of the year in 2013, and awarded the Presidential Medal of Freedom by President Barack Obama in 2016. He ranked 23rd on Rolling Stone's list of the Greatest Artists of All Time, which described him as being "the embodiment of rock and roll."

Peter Criss (Resides in Wall Township)

George Peter John Criscuola (born December 20, 1945), better known by his stage name Peter Criss, is a retired American musician, best known as a co-founder, original drummer, and vocalist of the hard rock band Kiss. Criss established The Catman character for his Kiss persona. In 2014, he was inducted into the Rock and Roll Hall of Fame as a member of Kiss.

Jon Bon Jovi (Born in Perth Amboy)

John Francis Bongiovi Jr. (born March 2, 1962), known professionally as Jon Bon Jovi, is an American singer, songwriter, guitarist, and actor. He is best known as the founder and front man of the rock band Bon Jovi, which was formed in 1983. He has released 15 studio albums with his band as well as two solo albums.

In the 1990s, Bon Jovi started an acting career, starring in the films Moonlight and Valentino and U-571 and appearing on television in Sex and the City, Ally McBeal, and The West Wing.

As a songwriter, Bon Jovi was inducted into the Songwriters Hall of Fame in 2009. In 2012, he ranked number 50 on the list of Billboard magazine's "Power 100" and ranking of "The Most Powerful and Influential People in the Music Business." In 1996, People magazine named him one of the "50 Most Beautiful People in the World." In 2000, People awarded him the title "Sexiest Rock Star."

Bon Jovi was a founder and former majority owner of the Arena Football League team, the Philadelphia Soul. He is the founder of The Jon Bon Jovi Soul Foundation, founded in 2006.

Debbie Harry (Resides in Red Bank)

Deborah Ann Harry (born Angela Trimble; July 1, 1945) is an American singer, songwriter and actress, best known as the lead vocalist of the band Blondie. Four of her songs with the band reached No.1 on the U.S. charts between 1979 and 1981.

Born in Miami, Florida, Harry was adopted as an infant and raised in Hawthorne, New Jersey. After attending college, she worked various jobs—as a dancer, a Playboy Bunny, and a secretary (including at the BBC in New York) before her breakthrough in the music industry. Harry co-formed Blondie in 1974 in New York City. The band released its eponymous debut album in 1976, and released a further three albums between then and 1979, including Parallel Lines, which spawned six singles, including "Heart of Glass." Their fifth album, Autoamerican (1980), afforded Harry and the band further attention, spawning such hits as a cover of "The Tide Is High" and "Rapture" which is considered the first rap song to chart at number one in the United States.

Thomas Pollock Anshutz (Vacationed in Holly Beach)

Thomas Pollock Anshutz (October 5, 1851 – June 16, 1912) was an American painter and teacher. Known for his portraiture and genre scenes, Anshutz was a co-founder of The Darby School. One of Thomas Eakins's most prominent students, he succeeded Eakins as director of drawing and painting classes at the Pennsylvania Academy of Fine Arts.

The Anshutz family regularly vacationed in Holly Beach, a borough that existed in Cape May County from 1885 to 1912, which served as a creative place for the painter

Jack Nicholson (Born in Neptune City)

John Joseph Nicholson (born April 22, 1937) is an American retired actor and filmmaker. He is widely regarded as one of the greatest actors of all time. In many of his films, he played rebels against the social structure. He received numerous accolades throughout his career which spanned over five decades, including three Academy Awards, three BAFTA Awards, six Golden Globe Awards, a Grammy Award, and a Screen Actors Guild Award. He's also received the American Film Institute's Life Achievement Award in 1994, and the Kennedy Center Honor in 2001.

Budd Abbott (Born in Asbury Park)

William Alexander "Bud" Abbott (October 2, 1897 – April 24, 1974) was an American comedian, actor, and producer. He was best known as the straight man half of the comedy duo Abbott and Costello.

Danny Devito (Born in Neptune Township)

Daniel Michael DeVito Jr. (born November 17, 1944) is an American actor, comedian, and filmmaker. He gained prominence for his portrayal of the taxi dispatcher Louie De Palma in the television series Taxi (1978–1983), which won him a Golden Globe Award and an Emmy Award. He plays Frank Reynolds on the FX and FXX sitcom It's Always Sunny in Philadelphia (2006–present).

He is known for his film roles in One Flew Over the Cuckoo's Nest (1975), Terms of Endearment (1983), Romancing the Stone (1984), Throw Momma from the Train (1987), Twins (1988), The War of the Roses (1989), Batman Returns (1992), Jack the Bear (1993), Junior (1994), Get Shorty (1995), Matilda (1996), L.A. Confidential (1997), The Big Kahuna (1999), Big Fish (2003), Deck the Halls (2006), When in Rome (2010), Wiener-Dog (2016) and Jumanji: The Next Level (2019). He is also known for his voice roles in such films as Hercules (1997), The Lorax (2012) and Smallfoot (2018).

Todd Frazier (Born in Point Pleasant)

Todd Brian Frazier (born February 12, 1986), nicknamed "The Toddfather," is an American former professional baseball third baseman. He played in Major League Baseball (MLB) for the Cincinnati Reds, Chicago White Sox, New York Yankees, Texas Rangers, New York Mets, and Pittsburgh Pirates. Frazier is 6'2", 215 lbs., and right-handed.

Soren Sorensen "Sam" Adams (Lived in Perth Amboy)

Soren Sorensen "Sam" Adams (May 24, 1879– October 20, 1963) was a Danish-American inventor and manufacturer of novelty products.

In 1928, Sam invented the prototype of what was to become the joy buzzer, a mechanical device placed in the hand, which emitted a loud vibrating buzz, when a button on the buzzer was depressed. This would usually occur when two people shook hands. He took the prototype to Dresden, Germany, where a tool and die maker created the tooling to make small parts for the item, which was now just 3.2 cm (1-1/4 inches) in diameter and 1.8 cm (3/4 inch) thick. The final item was patented in 1932. The success of the item allowed him to greatly increase his staff and purchase the former Symphonion music box factory building (constructed in 1893, demolished 2017) in Neptune, all during the Great Depression.

Steven Van Zandt (Lived in Middletown Township)

Steven Van Zandt (né Lento; born November 22, 1950), also known as Little Steven or Miami Steve, is an American musician, singer, songwriter, and actor. He is a member of Bruce Springsteen's E Street Band, in which he plays guitar and mandolin. He has appeared in several television drama series, including as Silvio Dante in The Sopranos (1999–2007) and as Frank Tagliano in Lilyhammer (2012–2014). Van Zandt has his own solo band called Little Steven and The Disciples of Soul, intermittently active since the 1980s. In 2014, he was inducted into the Rock and Roll Hall of Fame as a member of the E Street Band. Van Zandt has produced music, written songs, and had his own songs covered by Bruce Springsteen, Meat Loaf, Nancy Sinatra, Pearl Jam, Artists United Against Apartheid, and the Iron City Houserockers, among others.

William James "Count" Basie (Born in Red Bank)

William James "Count" Basie (/ˈbeɪsi/; August 21, 1904 – April 26, 1984) was an American jazz pianist, organist, bandleader, and composer. In 1935, he formed the Count Basie Orchestra, and in 1936 took them to Chicago for a long engagement and their first recording. He led the group for almost 50 years, creating innovations like the use of two "split" tenor saxophones, emphasizing the rhythm section, riffing with a big band, using arrangers to broaden their sound, and others. Many musicians came to prominence under his direction, including the tenor saxophonists Lester Young and Herschel Evans, the guitarist Freddie Green, trumpeters Buck Clayton and Harry "Sweets" Edison, plunger trombonist Al Grey, and singers Jimmy Rushing, Helen Humes, Thelma Carpenter, and Joe Williams.

Khigh Dhiegh (Born in Spring Lake)

Khigh Alx Dhiegh (/ˈkaɪˈdiː/KYDEE or /ˈdeɪ/DAY; born Kenneth Dickerson; August 25, 1910 – October 25, 1991) was an American television and motion picture actor of Anglo-Egyptian Sudanese ancestry, noted for portraying East Asian roles. He is perhaps best remembered for portraying villains, in particular his recurring TV guest role as Chinese

agent Wo Fat on Hawaii Five-O (from the pilot in 1968 to the final episode in 1980), and brainwashing expert Dr. Yen Lo in 1962's The
Manchurian Candidate.

Leavander Johnson (Born in Atlantic City)

Leavander Johnson (December 24, 1969 – September 22, 2005) was
an American lightweight boxer from Atlantic City, who once held the
International Boxing Federation version of the world title. He won the
title on June 17, 2005, against the Italian fighter Stefano Zoff, winning
after the referee stopped the fight in the seventh round. Johnson lost his
first IBF title defense. After walking out of the ring following that fight,
he collapsed in the locker room and died of brain injuries several days
later.

Kurt Loder (Born in Ocean City)

Kurtis Loder (born May 5, 1945) is an American entertainment
critic, author, columnist, and television personality. He served in the
1980s as editor at Rolling Stone, during a tenure that Reason later called
"legendary." He has contributed to articles in Reason, Esquire, Details,
New York, and Time. He has also made cameos on several films and
television series. He is best known for his role at MTV News since the
1980s and for appearing in other MTV-related television specials. He has
hosted the SiriusXM radio show True Stories since 2016.

Russell Louis "Rusty" Schweickart (Born in Neptune)

Russell Louis "Rusty" Schweickart (also Schweikart; born October
25, 1935) is an American aeronautical engineer, and a former NASA astronaut, research scientist, U.S. Air Force fighter pilot, as well as a former business executive and government executive.

Schweickart was selected in 1963 for NASA's third astronaut group.
He was the Lunar Module Pilot on the 1969 Apollo 9 mission, the first
crewed flight test of the lunar module, on which he performed the first
in-space test of the portable life support system used by the Apollo as-
tronauts who walked on the Moon. As backup Commander of the first
crewed Skylab mission in 1973, he was responsible for developing the
hardware and procedures used by the first crew to perform critical in-

flight repairs of the Skylab station. After Skylab, he served for a time as Director of User Affairs in NASA's Office of Applications.

Schweickart left NASA in 1977 to serve for two years as California Governor Jerry Brown's assistant for science and technology, then was appointed by Brown to California's Energy Commission for five and a half years, serving as chairman for three.

In 1984–85 he co-founded the Association of Space Explorers and later in 2002 co-founded the B612 Foundation, a non-profit organization dedicated to defending Earth from asteroid impacts, along with fellow former astronaut Ed Lu and two planetary scientists. He served for a period as its chair before becoming its chair emeritus.

Norman Mailer (Born in Long Branch)

Nachem Malech Mailer (January 31, 1923 – November 10, 2007), known by his pen name Norman Kingsley Mailer, was an American novelist, journalist, playwright, filmmaker, and actor. In a career spanning over six decades, Mailer had 11 best-selling books, at least one in each of the seven decades after World War II.

His novel The Naked and the Dead was published in 1948 and brought him early renown. His 1968 nonfiction novel Armies of the Night won the Pulitzer Prize for non-fiction as well as the National Book Award. Among his best-known works is The Executioner's Song, the 1979 winner of the Pulitzer Prize for fiction.

Frank Pallone, Jr. Member of Congress

Frank Pallone Jr. is, first and foremost, the congressman from the Jersey Shore. To drive home that point, his name shows up in the news every year as the guy who helps replenish the sand on its beaches—an estimated total of 163 million cubic yards of the stuff over the last three decades, at a cost of $1.2 billion to the federal government. The lifelong Long Branch resident has served since 1988 in the House of Representatives, and has been chairman of the powerful Energy and Commerce Committee since the Democratic Party took back control of the House last year.

Trivia

Perth Amboy

- The earliest residents of Perth Amboy were the Lenape Native Americans who called the point on which the city lies "Ompoge."

- The area was dubbed New Perth in 1684 in honor of James Drummond who was an associate of a major Scottish proprietary and considered the Earl of Perth.

- In 1684, Perth Amboy became the capital of East Jersey and remained the capital until the union of East and West Jersey in 1702.

- The Raritan Yacht Club in Perth Amboy is one of the oldest yacht clubs in the United States.

- In 1914, Perth Amboy had a baseball team called the Pacers. They only played for one season.

- Local attractions include the Perth Amboy Ferry Slip, two small museums, an art gallery, a yacht club, and a marina.

- Since 1939, legal use of a bicycle in Perth Amboy requires a license issued by the Perth Amboy police department.

- Perth Amboy City Hall is the oldest in use in the United States.

- Perth Amboy is usually regarded as the place where the first African American person, Thomas Mundt Peterson, voted (March 31, 1870) in the United States.

South Amboy

- Founded in 1798, South Amboy is located along the Raritan River, south of Staten Island and across the river from Perth Amboy.

- Scenes from the 2000 film "Coyote Ugly" were filmed in South Amboy and the main character is from the city.

- In 1932 John Stevens built the first railroad in New Jersey running between Camden and South Amboy.

Laurence Harbor (Old Bridge)

- The lands known today as Laurence Harbor were part of the southernmost region inhabited by the Lenni Lenape tribe, also known as the Delaware, in the 17th century.

- Laurence Harbor is named after land developer Laurence Lamb, who bought property in (what was then known as) Madison Township at the turn of the 20th century and subdivided it into bungalow-sized lots.

- Laurence Harbor was considered a beach resort back in the 1920s to 1950s.

- Except for a few cold winter months, egrets can be seen frequently in the area.

- Along the boardwalk amongst the sand dunes, there are honeysuckle trees that blossom in the spring.

Keansburg

- Keansburg was formed as a borough by an act of the New Jersey Legislature on March 26, 1917, from portions of both Middletown Township and Raritan Township (now Hazlet), based on the results of a referendum held on April 17, 1917.

- In 1904 William Gehlhaus convinced five investors to join him in purchasing the area of marshland overlooking Raritan Bay in hopes of creating a resort area.

- Keansburg is best known for its amusement park.

Atlantic Highlands

- The Borough of Atlantic Highlands, once known as Portland Pointe, was originally part of Middletown Township.

- The major construction occurred from the 1880s through 1900. It included hotels, cottages, rooming houses, and private homes.

- Atlantic Highlands was a haven for bootleggers during the Prohibition era.

- Atlantic Highlands Recreation Committee runs many events in town throughout the year including a Summer Concert Series in the harbor, youth programs such as basketball in the winter and soccer in the fall.

- Atlantic Highlands' Sea streak Ferry can take you to Wall Street in 40 minutes.

Sandy Hook

- Built in 1764, the Sandy Hook Lighthouse is the oldest standing lighthouse in the country.

- Sandy Hook is home to Fort Hancock, a Nike Missile Base, and multiple hidden historical landmarks.

- Cactus can be found on a Sandy Hook nature walk. You may also spot horseshoe crabs and seals.

- Gunnison Beach in Sandy Hook is "clothing optional."

Red Bank

- Red Bank has been occupied by indigenous people for thousands of years.

- Originally part of "Shrewsbury Towne," Red Bank was named in 1736 when Thomas Morford sold Joseph French "a lot of over three acres on the west side of the highway that goes to the red bank."

- By 1844 Red Bank had become a commercial and manufacturing center focused on textiles, tanning, furs, and other goods for sale in Manhattan.

- Downtown Red Bank is known for its many local and well-known businesses including Garmany, Urban Outfitters, and Tiffany & Co, on and around Broad St.

- Red Bank's many annual events include the International Beer, Wine & Food Festival; a long-running sidewalk sale; a farmer's market; an indie film festival; the Red Bank Guinness Oyster Festival; a Halloween parade; and a holiday town lighting.

- Red Bank is known for its artistic activity and is home to the Monmouth County Arts Council as well as several art and photography galleries.

- Many venues in Red Bank have live performances, plays, and movie showings.

- The classic landmark hotel, Molly Pitcher Inn, was named after Mary Hays from the Revolutionary War. The hotel offers fine dining and has several rooms to host social events.

- The restaurant Soul Kitchen has no prices on the menu but accepts donations. It was opened by New Jersey rocker Jon Bon Jovi, designed for people who can't normally afford to eat out.

Deal

- Deal is a borough in Monmouth County, in the U.S. state of New Jersey, settled by Europeans in the mid-1660s and named after an English carpenter from Deal, Kent.

- Eighty percent of Deal's population are Sephardic Jews.

- In 2022 Deal ranked as New Jersey's most expensive zip code with homes valued at $2,400,000.

Oceanport

- The land making up today's Oceanport was settled as part of the Monmouth Patent, a purchase agreement approved by royal Governor Richard Nicholls in 1665.

- Oceanport is a river town, but throughout the 1700s, shipping was vital since the town had access to the ocean via the river it's on.

- The town's fortunes improved when Monmouth Park Racetrack was opened in 1870 along the western side of town.

Long Branch

- Long Branch emerged as a beach resort town in the late 18th century, named for its location along a branch of the South Shrewsbury River.

- Long Branch takes its name from the "long branch" or south branch of the Shrewsbury River.

- During its heyday in the 19th century, Long Branch was a resort town that for the "Who's Who" of society.

- Seven Presidents Oceanfront Park is named for the first seven U.S. presidents who vacationed there. The park comprises thirty-eight acres and offers an ocean beach, swimming, fishing, boating, volleyball plus a boardwalk.

- Long Branch's Pier Village is an award-winning mixed-use beachfront Victorian-inspired community which features over thirty notable restaurants as well as shopping.

Asbury Park

- Asbury Park was developed in 1871 as a residential resort by New York brush manufacturer James A. Bradley.

- Asbury Park was named for Francis Asbury, the first American bishop of the Methodist Episcopal Church in the United States.

- In the 1920s, Paramount Theatre and Convention Hall complex, the Casino Arena and Carousel House, and two handsome red-brick pavilions were built in the Asbury Boardwalk area.

- Asbury Park was the first Jersey Shore town to have a municipal sewer system.

- In 1943, the New York Yankees held their spring training in Asbury Park instead of Florida.

- The Asbury Park exit on the Garden State Parkway opened in 1956.

- In 1965, Margaret Hogan, a former nun, opened the groundbreaking lesbian club, Chez Elle (French for "her house").

- The Stone Pony, founded in 1974, was a starting point for many musicians.

- After Hurricane Sandy, Asbury Park was one of the few communities on the Jersey Shore to reopen successfully for the 2013 summer season.

- The New Jersey Music Hall of Fame was founded in Asbury Park in 2005.

Ocean Grove

- On July 31, 1869, Reverend W. B. Osborn, Reverend Stokes, and other Methodist ministers camped at a shaded, well-drained spot, on New Jersey's seashore, and decided to establish a permanent Christian camp meeting community called "Ocean Grove."

- Ocean Grove's Great Auditorium, constructed in 1894, is acclaimed as "the state's most wondrous wooden structure, soaring and sweeping, alive with the sound of music." Famed conductor, Leonard Bernstein once compared it to Carnegie Hall.

- From May to September of each year, 114 tents are erected around the Great Auditorium to form "Tent City" a tradition of the Camp Meeting Association that dates back to 1869.

- In 1975, Ocean Grove was designated a State and National Historic District as a 19th-century planned urban community. It has the most extensive collection of Victorian and early-20th century architecture in the United States.

- Until 1979, you couldn't drive in Ocean Grove on Sundays.

- Ocean Grove is a dry town. No liquor can be sold in Ocean Grove.

- Sabbath prohibits the driving of cars and trucks on Sundays.

Neptune Township

- The Township of Neptune was named for the Roman water deity, and its location on the Atlantic Ocean.

- Essex Road, which runs through Tinton Falls and Neptune, is known for tales of ghosts lurking in the woods.

- Neptune City had one church, the Memorial United Methodist Church. As of 2023, the building was permanently closed and for sale.

Avon-by-the Sea

- Avon-by-the-Sea was incorporated as a borough by an act of the New Jersey Legislature on March 23, 1900, from portions of Neptune City.

- Avon-by-the-Sea is best known for its clean, white, sandy beaches. Year-round activities include boating and scuba diving.

- Avon-by-the-Sea can be reveled in during off-season, as the non-commercial boardwalk is abounding with Victorian lamps, benches, and pavilions.

Belmar

- Belmar mean "beautiful sea" in Italian.

- Belmar is known for several annual events including their Sand Castle Contest, their St. Patrick's Day Parade, their Pro Surf Contest, and their Sprint Triathlon.

- Belmar is home to the first and oldest first-aid squad in the United States.

- Belmar's "E" Street is the original source of Bruce Springsteen's "E Street Band."

- In the HBO series, "The Sopranos," Belmar is shown as the home port of Tony Soprano's boat, the Stugots.

- American restauranteur, Guy Fieri, featured Belmar and local restaurant 10th Avenue Burrito in an episode of Food Network's "Diner's Drive-Ins, and Dives."

Spring Lake

- During the "Gilded Age" of the late 19th and early 20th centuries, Spring Lake developed into a coastal resort for members of New York City and Philadelphia high society, in similar fashion to the settlements of Newport, Rhode Island and Bar Harbor, Maine.

- This small beach resort area consisting of beautiful parks and Victorian homes is sometimes warmly called "The Irish Riviera."

- Even during the summer's peak season, you will find very few people and almost no traffic in Spring Lake. Even the long, non-commercial boardwalk is peaceful.

- Spring Lake's downtown is made up of upscale boutiques, cafes, and restaurants. There are no souvenir shops or chain stores.

Sea Girt

- Sea Girt was named by Commodore Stockton after he purchased land in the area in 1853. But long before the white man settled in on this Jersey Shore spot, the Lenni Lenape Indians inhabited the area.

- Sea Girt Light began operation on December 10, 1896, and is located on Ocean Avenue and Beacon Boulevard.

- Sea Girt's beaches and boardwalk are open all year long, with full time lifeguards on duty from Father's Day until Labor Day

Manasquan

- The Algonquin Arts Theatre is a Manasquan landmark which has shown and movies throughout the year. It's a historic 540-seat theatre built in 1938 as a movie house and was converted to a professional live performance space in May 1994.

- Manasquan was once a tourist destination and has turned into a year-round community due to the demolition of traditional beach

115

bungalows and having lost many of the bars once located in its borders.

- The Fireman's' Fair, which dates back to 1974, with the exception of a decade-long hiatus from the late 1990s until 2011, occurs every July/August.

- Until 2010 Manasquan was home to the Cat Fanciers' Association (CFA), the largest registry of pedigreed cats in the world.

Point Pleasant Beach

- The Point Pleasant Beach area was first occupied by the Lenape Native Americans.

- The Point Pleasant boardwalk spans a mile long and is made up of mostly amusement rides, the Jenkinson's Aquarium, pizza joints, ice cream parlors, games, and miniature golf courses. You can also find sushi.

- Each September, Point Pleasant Beach hosts an annual Seafood Festival.

- Point Pleasant Beach was one of the numerous Jersey Shore communities that was devastated by Hurricane Sandy in October 2012.

- Composer Edward Manukyan, who lived in Point Pleasant Beach briefly in 2002, wrote the song "Point Pleasant Beach" about the borough.

Seaside Park

- The first inhabitants of the Seaside Park barrier island were Lenape Native Americans who came in search of fish, crabs, clams, and scallops. They called the area "Seheyichbi," which meant "land bordering the ocean."

- Sharing its border with Seaside Heights, Seaside Park is the calmer of the two. It has its own boardwalk, but there are no rides or arcades.

- A Seaside Park favorite is Uncle Nick's Sub Shop, in business for over 30 years.

Seaside Heights

- Seaside Heights is a resort community, made popular by the beach, an amusement-oriented boardwalk, and numerous bars and clubs.

- Seaside Heights is known as the location of the MTV hit show, "Jersey Shore" which was an economic benefit to the town, according to the director of the borough's business improvement district.

- The two boardwalk amusement park piers at Seaside Heights are Casino Pier and Funtown Pier. They offer many family-friendly attractions ranging from arcades to games of chance, to beaches, and to the wide variety of foods and desserts, all within walking distance.

- In 1985 New Jersey rock band Bon Jovi filmed most of their music video for the song, "In and Out of Love" in Seaside Heights, on the boardwalk.

- The ABC soap opera, "One Life to Live" filmed a portion of its 2008 storyline in Seaside Heights, on the beach and boardwalk.

- In the summer at Seaside Heights, there is free seaside entertainment which includes movies on the beach, concerts, and weekly fireworks displays.

- Seaside Heights is noted for their annual Polar Bear Plunge, where swimmers go into the icy cold Atlantic during winter in order to raise money for the Special Olympics.

Ortley Beach

- The current location of Ortley Beach was once home to Cranberry Inlet, an important maritime route that closed after an 1812 storm.

- Ortley Beach was settled as a vacation resort in the 1940s and 1950s.

- Ortley Beach is a small, quiet, seaside vacation destination, less than a square mile in size. The beach is the main attraction.

Toms River

- European settlers first arrived in the area between 1614 and 1685. In 1685, the British-born Thomas Luker settled along the banks of what was then called Goose Creek. Luker began operating a small ferry service across the waterway, which eventually became known as Toms River.

- Joshua Huddy Park is located in Downtown Toms River and is host to a replica constructed in 1931 of the Revolutionary War fort that was once standing near the site.

- Toms River is featured in various TV and news media, including MTV's "Made" and "Jersey Shore," HBO's "Boardwalk Empire" and the original "The Amityville Horror" movie.

- In 1998 Toms River East Little League won the Little League World Series.

- Toms River has the second-largest Halloween parade in the world.

- Toms River has many shopping malls including Ocean County Mall (the only enclosed mall in Ocean County and the Seacourt Pavilion, located across Bay Avenue from the Ocean County Mall.

Lavallette

- Lavallette was named for Elie A. F. La Vallette, one of the first rear admirals appointed in the United States Navy when President Abraham Lincoln created the rank in July 1862, and the father of Albert T. Lavallette, co-founder of the borough.

- The borough of Lavallette offers tennis, bocce, shuffleboard, basketball, and roller blading opportunities on land; and by sea, there's fishing, crabbing, swimming, boating, sailing, windsurfing, and other water sports.

- Lavallette entertainment includes band concerts, fireworks, and Movies on the Bay, held at the Centennial Gazebo and Gardens located at Philadelphia Avenue and the bayfront.

Bay Head

- The Bayhead Land Company was incorporated on September 6, 1879, capitalized at $12,000. The founding partners of Bay Head were David H. Mount of Rocky Hill, and three Princeton men: Edward Howe, his brother Leavitt Howe and William Harris.

- Bay Head's historic district is architecturally significant for its large collection of well-preserved Shingle Style, Stick Style, and Queen Anne Style structures.

- Bay Head is less than a square mile and everything is within walking distance—the beach, restaurants, a wine and cheese shop, a bakery, public tennis courts, gift shops, bed and breakfasts, and a bank.

- Bay Head has no bars, nor a commercial boardwalk.

Long Beach Island

- Long Beach Island is colloquially known as LBI, The LBI Region, or simply The Island. It's approximately eighteen miles in length.

119

- The island has been continuously settled since 1690, initially being a destination for hunters.

- Long Beach Island typically attracts a family-oriented crowd during the summer. Visitors enjoy miniature golf, parasailing, jet-skiing, walking, shopping, and relaxing on the beaches. There are many bars, and some feature live music, DJs, and happy hour.

Surf City

- Surf City is a highly popular portion of Long Beach Island. It's "Boulevard" section features plenty of shopping and restaurants.

- Present-day Surf City was home to one of the first big boarding hotels on the Jersey Shore, called the Mansion of Health.

- The Surf City Yacht Club participates in weekly races against other yacht clubs throughout the island, with many sailors and swimmers ranging in age.

Atlantic City

- Atlantic City was incorporated in 1854, the same year train service began on the Camden and Atlantic Railroad.

- The Atlantic City Boardwalk was built in 1870 along a portion of the beach in an effort to help hotel owners keep sand out of their lobbies.

- In 1883 salt-water taffy was conceived in Atlantic City by David Bradley.

- Atlantic City, sometimes referred to by its initials A.C., is a coastal resort city in Atlantic County. It's known for its casinos, boardwalk, and beaches.

- Atlantic City inspired the U.S. version of the board game Monopoly, which uses various Atlantic City street names and destinations in the game.

- Since 1921 Atlantic City has been the home of the Miss American pageant.

- In 1976 New Jersey voters legalized casino gambling in Atlantic City, and the first casino opened in 1978.

- Notable Atlantic City attractions include the Boardwalk Hall, House of Blues, and the famous Ripley's Believe It or Not museum.

Ventnor City

- Ventnor City it takes its name from another seaside resort in England.

- Ventnor City was among the first communities in the United States to be developed as an automobile suburb, a community that was developed for people who owned cars.

- The Ventnor City Boardwalk is one of the Jersey Shore's gems that offers an amazing view of the Atlantic Ocean.

Brigantine

- Brigantine has been called "the best beach on the New Jersey shore" because of its clean sand, fresh ocean air, and beautiful summer weather.

- Brigantine points of interest include Brigantine Lighthouse and The Brigantine Hotel.

- Brigantine Castle was once a popular funhouse and haunted house attraction by the beach in Brigantine. Constructed in 1976, it drew millions of visitors annually until it was damaged in a 1982 storm.

Ocean City

- Known as a family-oriented seaside resort, Ocean City has not allowed the sale of alcoholic beverages within its limits since its founding in 1879.

- In 1881, the first school on the island opened.

- In 1965, the Wonderland Amusement Park opened on the boardwalk at 6th Street, which is now known as Gillian's Wonderland Pier.

- The Ocean City Music Pier opened in 1929, and is still in full swing, as home to notable comedians and performers, as well as musical productions.

- The Stainton Wildlife Refuge is an incredible place to go for bird watchers.

Margate City

- Unlike other seashore towns, Margate has no hotels. Those who choose to visit in the summer are usually residents with second homes.

- Margate is the home of Lucy the Elephant, the "largest elephant in the world" and is the oldest remaining example of zoomorphic architecture left in the United States. Over 130 years old, she has been painstakingly restored and is toured by thousands of fans each year.

- Each summer Margate hosts "Beachstock." It's the largest beach party at the Jersey Shore!

Sea Isle City

- Sea Isle City was founded in 1882 by Charles K. Landis, who was also the founder of Vineland, New Jersey.

- The "Sara the Turtle Festival" is one of the city's annual festivals, celebrating a fictional turtle named Sara. Aimed towards families with young children, the festival features live animal exhibits and face painting meant to educate children about the local environment.

- During the summer, an outdoor Band Shell located in the heart of the downtown beachfront district offers free entertainment such as concerts, family dance parties, Movies Under the Stars, and "Sea Isle City's Got Talent" contests.

North Wildwood

- In the early 1600s, the Lenni Lenape Indians visited North Wildwood each summer to fish, relax and cool off on these beaches.

- The Wildwoods' beaches stretch for five miles across the shores of North Wildwood, Wildwood, and Wildwood Crest. They are wide, clean, and free!

- Cool Scoops Ice Cream in North Wildwood has hosted music legends like Bobby Rydell, Chubby Checker, Mary Wilson of the Supremes, and Buddy Holly's original Crickets.

Wildwood

- "Rock Around the Clock," often credited as the first rock and roll record, was first performed on Memorial Day weekend in 1954 at the HofBrau Hotel in Wildwood by Bill Haley & His Comets. The song's status as one of the first rock and roll hits has given rise to the city's claim as "the birthplace of rock and roll."

- Chubby Checker introduced his version of "The Twist" at the Rainbow Club in Wildwood.

- On occasion, American Bandstand broadcast from the Wildwood's Starlight Ballroom.

- Bobby Rydell's major hit, "Wildwood Days" in 1963, is about Wildwood.

- Murals in the Wildwood community honor Checker, Bill Haley; and Bobby Rydell.

- Wildwood is home to over 200 motels, built during the Doo-Wop era of the 1950s and 1960s. The term "doo-wop" was coined by Cape May's Mid-Atlantic Center for the Arts in the early 1990s to describe the unique, space-age architectural style, which is also referred to as the "Googie" or "populuxe" style. The motels are unique in appearance, with Vegas-like neon signs and fantastic architecture.

- A Wildwood 1950s Doo-Wop Museum includes property from demolished motels such as neon signs and furniture. In June 2006, its Doo-Wop-style motels were placed on the National Trust for Historic Preservation's annual Eleven Most Endangered List, described as "irreplaceable icons of popular culture."

- The boardwalk features a trolley called the "Tramcar," which runs from end to end.

- Boardwalk Chapel is a summertime Christian Gospel outreach on the boardwalk, sandwiched between a pizzeria and a gift shop. Visitors to the boardwalk are invited to attend any of its 77 consecutive evening services held during June, July, and August.

- A portion of the rock band Kiss's 1975 album Alive! was recorded from a July 23, 1975 concert at the old Wildwoods Convention Center.

Wildwood Crest

- In Wildwood Crest, several "Doo Wop" motels, such as the Caribbean Motel, are registered on the National Register of Historic Places. In recent years, historic "Doo Wop" motels have been demolished to make way for the construction of condominiums, leading to organized efforts to preserve the remaining examples.

- Part of the Wildwood Crest borough's beachfront has been closed off for the protection of native birds such as the piping plover. These small birds have this area all to themselves so that their eggs may be protected from beachgoers.

- Wildwood Crest is a dry town which joins Cape May Point and Ocean City among municipalities in Cape May restricting the sale of alcohol.

Avalon

- The Avalon area was purchased by Aaron Leaming in December 1722 for seventy-nine pounds.

- The Avalon community is one of the most affluent communities along the Jersey Shore and is home to some of the most expensive real estate on the East Coast. The Washingtonian, a monthly magazine distributed in Washington, D.C. named Avalon the "chicest beach" in the mid-Atlantic, the place to see women in diamonds and designer swimwear.

- Kohler's Bakery, known for serving baked items made from scratch, has been a part of the community of Avalon since 1949.

Cape May

- Cape May was founded in 1620 by Captain Cornelius Jacobsen Mey, a Dutch navigator.

- Cape May is the oldest seaside resort in America and is also known as the "Queen of the Seaside Resorts."

- Cape May is home to the largest collection of Victorian homes in America, many of which are open to the public for tours.

- The Cape May Lighthouse, built in 1859, is the third oldest operating lighthouse in the country.

- The Cape May Point State Park offers visitors a chance to see a wide variety of migratory birds and other wildlife.

- Cape May is home to the Mid-Atlantic Center for the Arts & Humanities, which offers a wide range of tours, events, and programs that focus on the city's history and culture.

- Cape May is also a popular spot for fishing and boating. Popular species include flounder, striped bass, and bluefish.

- Cape May is home to the Naval Air Station Wildwood Aviation Museum, which features exhibits on the military history of the area.

- Cape May is home to the Cape May Music Festival, an annual event featuring a wide range of classical and jazz performances.

- Cape May is known for its Victorian architecture, which is why it's also known as "the nation's first seaside resort."

Do You Know "Jersey Shore" the Television Show?

Many fans of the hit TV show Jersey Shore are familiar with its wild antics and outrageous cast of characters. But there are some facts about this iconic series that even the most die-hard viewers may not know!

For instance, did you know that during its run, the show was filmed in eleven different locations- spanning New York, New Jersey, Florida, and Italy? This is likely because producers wanted to capture a wide range of different life experiences for their viewers.

Another lesser-known fact is that when it first premiered in 2009, it was actually one of MTV's lowest rated shows ever. However, thanks to an increase in popularity over time (and a lot of clever marketing!) it quickly became one of their most successful programs ever with millions tuning in every week.

Did you know that the show was filmed in an actual house? It's true! The Seaside Heights home served as the primary filming location for all six seasons of the show and has become something of a tourist attraction in recent years.

The real estate company that owns the house also keeps it in pristine condition - despite requests from members of the public to purchase or rent out rooms. It's unclear if this request is due to sentimental value or simply just because they want a piece of Jersey Shore history!

Another closely guarded secret is how much money each cast member made during their tenure on the show. While exact figures are unknown, reports suggest that some may have earned up to $15,000 per episode—an impressive sum for any aspiring reality stars!

Another secret about Jersey Shore is that many iconic locations used during filming still remain popular tourist spots today. From Seaside Heights Boardwalk to "Sammi's Sweet Shop" (which was actually just a set piece!), these places continue to draw thousands each year as part of their "Jersey Shore Pilgrimage".

Jersey Shore Lighthouses

The Absecon Lighthouse

It is New Jersey's tallest lighthouse, first lit in 1857. It is no longer in service and now is a It is a venue for weddings, both small and large. The country's third tallest Lighthouse it is located in Atlantic City and open for climbing.

Cape May Lighthouse — Cape May

Located at the southern tip of New Jersey, Cape May Lighthouse is a wonderful destination with plenty for kids to do. Nautical-themed Lighthouse Storytimes are held on Saturday at 12:30 p.m. from Memorial Day to Labor Day. Family Fun Days take place every Wednesday in July and August. Kids can also climb the lighthouse's 199 steps or check out the many attractions available in Cape May Point State Park.

Hereford Inlet Lighthouse — North Wildwood

Hereford Inlet Lighthouse is truly picturesque. Surrounded by beautiful English country gardens that are home to more than two hundred plant varieties, the lighthouse itself looks like a darling Victorian cottage. Your kids will love chasing butterflies in the garden and watching squirrels at the feeding station. In addition to being a working lighthouse, Hereford is also a museum. Tour the grounds and get a glimpse of an early 20th-century lighthouse keeper's life.

Sandy Hook Lighthouse — Sandy Hook

The oldest operating lighthouse in the United States, Sandy Hook Lighthouse was lit for the first time in 1764. Surrounded by Fort Hancock and part of Gateway National Recreation Area, it's a great location for a family trip. Tour the Lighthouse and Keepers Quarters. Open year round, lighthouse tours are first come, first served, from 1–4:30 p.m. Kids must be at least 48" tall to climb the tower. Admission is free.

Sea Girt Lighthouse — Sea Girt

Sea Girt Lighthouse was constructed in 1896 to bridge the gap between the Barnegat and Navesink Lighthouses after numerous shipwrecks. The last live-in lighthouse built on the Atlantic Coast, it was in disrepair until leased by the Sea Girt Lighthouse Citizens Committee in 1981 and subsequently restored. Free tours are offered Sundays 2–4 p.m., except holiday weekends, April thru November 19.

Twin Lights — Highlands

The unique dual tower design of the Twin Lights makes it a must-see for lighthouse aficionados. Climbers to the top of the North Tower will be treated to stunning views of the Atlantic Ocean. The on-site museum exhibits lighthouse and lifesaving station artifacts, as well as many educational programs for visitors.

Barnegat Lighthouse

The site of the Barnegat Lighthouse on the northern tip of Long Beach Island in Ocean County was considered one of the most crucial "change of Course" points for vessels going to and from New York. Lt. George G Meade, an Army Engineer and Union General in the Civil War designed the new $60,000 Lighthouse in 1855. The current Coast Guard approved lens creates a single beam that can be seen up to twenty-two nautical miles. The original lens is on display at the Barnegat Lighthouse Historical Society Museum.

Hurricane Sandy

On October 29, 2012, about two and a half hours from its New Jersey landfall, Hurricane Sandy transitioned into an extratropical cyclone as it encountered cooler waters and a cold air mass. At about 6:30 p.m., the center of former hurricane Sandy made landfall near Brigantine in Atlantic County, with maximum sustained winds of about 80 mph. The highest wind gust in the state was 91 mph in Atlantic City. At the Atlantic City Marina, a barometer recorded a minimum barometric pressure of 945.5 mbar, which set a record for the city, and was the lowest pressure ever recorded in the United States north of North Carolina. Sandy dropped heavy rainfall across the state as it approached and later moved across the state. The statewide peak precipitation total was 11.91 inches, recorded in Wildwood Crest. This made it the sixth wettest tropical cyclone in the state.

The most damaging aspects of Sandy were from its high waves, estimated from 12 to 24 ft., as well as its storm surge, which is the rise in water above the normally expected high tide. Record-high water levels occurred in the state due to the storm's fast motion toward the coast and its passage during the regular high tide. The highest water levels occurred north of the landfall point in Monmouth and Middlesex Counties, especially along the Raritan Bay, where the surge reached an estimated 4 to 9 ft. Along Sandy Hook at the northern end of Monmouth County, a tide gauge on a pier recorded a water level of 13.31 ft. above the average low tide, at which point the pier collapsed and the gauge stopped reporting. This indicated a storm surge of 8.57 ft., which broke the previous record high tide there by 2.87 ft., set by Hurricane Donna in 1960. The highest high water mark in the state was 8.9 ft., measured at the Coast Guard station in Sandy Hook. The most significant flooding in the state occurred in the areas around Lower New York Bay, Raritan Bay, and the Raritan River. Along the Jersey Shore, the high water levels inundated several barrier islands, with a new temporary inlet created in Mantoloking. Most coastal towns in New Jersey suffered beach erosion due to Sandy's waves, and on average, beaches were 30 to 40 ft. (9.1 to 12.2 m) narrower after the storm. However, some beaches in the extreme southern end of the state grew in size. As Sandy entered Pennsylvania, a strong southeasterly flow produced record flooding along the Delaware Bay and Delaware River.

Across New Jersey, 38 people died due in part to Sandy, including 12 fatalities directly related to the hurricane's impacts. The large swath of strong winds and widespread flooding produced the costliest natural disaster in the history of New Jersey, with damage estimated at $29.4 billion. This far surpassed the $1 billion damage total Hurricane Irene from the 2011, the state's previous costliest natural disaster. Damage was heaviest in Ocean and Monmouth counties. Statewide, Sandy damaged 346,000 homes, with about 30,000 homes and businesses damaged or significantly damaged. The storm's high winds and heavy rainfall knocked down or damaged more than 113,000 trees across the state, many of which fell onto power lines, leaving about 2.7 million New Jerseyans without power. The power outages affected 70 water systems and 80 sewage systems. High waters sank 1400 boats.

Flooding and Damage in Atlantic City

An analysis of aerial imagery conducted by the Federal Emergency Management Agency (FEMA) indicated that approximately 72,000 homes and business in New Jersey were damaged or destroyed by the storm, with over 40,000 of the buildings affected being in Ocean County. Based on this analysis, 507 buildings were destroyed, 5051 suffered major structural damage, and 66,212 incurred limited damage. U.S. Congressman Chris Smith stated on January 2, 2013, that 346,000 homes in New Jersey were damaged by Sandy, of which 22,000 were rendered uninhabitable.

Recovery Efforts

Ten years after Hurricane Sandy, many towns on the Jersey Shore have come back stronger than ever. Towns like Ocean Beach in Toms River, Manahawkin/Stafford Township, Seaside Heights, Highlands, Wildwood Crest and North Wildwood have all seen tremendous recovery efforts since the storm.

In Ocean Beach, homes were rebuilt with federal aid and the town has been able to scramble for revenue to support itself. In Manahawkin/Stafford Township, residents say that while the community still feels like a ghost town in some areas, homeowners have been able to make progress in their recovery efforts. Seaside Heights has experienced a transformation since Sandy with more than 46% of borough homes being rebuilt or repaired.

Highlands was hit hard by the storm but has seen an influx of wealthy buyers who are attracted to its waterfront views and post-Sandy building regulations that require new construction to be elevated above flood levels. Wildwood Crest and North Wildwood have kept their beaches free for all despite suffering from beach erosion due to Sandy's waves.

The state of New Jersey as a whole has bounced back from the storm but recovery was not even across all towns on the Jersey Shore. Some areas are still struggling due to lack of resources or funding while other areas have made great strides in rebuilding and strengthening their communities against future storms.

Do You Know?

High floodwaters temporarily **cut off travel** between the city and the mainland.

High waves **destroyed the northern end of the Atlantic City boardwalk**, which was already scheduled to be removed.

In the city, more than **5000 housing units were damaged during Sandy**, which represented 11 percent of the statewide number of damaged units.

Part of the **Ocean City-Longport Bridge** was closed when high seas washed boulders onto it.

In Ocean County, located north of Atlantic County, **damage was severest** in the eastern portion of the county, including Long Beach Island, the Barnegat Peninsula, and along the Barnegat Bay. Damage in the county was worst along the Barnegat Peninsula, with parts of Seaside Park inundated by 4.4 feet of floodwaters.

Mantoloking created a temporary inlet and swept away several homes, with such severe damage that residents were not allowed to move back until February 2013, or about three months after the storm. Also in

Mantoloking, ruptured natural gas lines ignited fires, destroying 14 homes.

In **Seaside Heights**, toward the southern end of the Barnegat Peninsula, the storm washed away a 50 foot portion of Fun Pier, a local amusement park.

A portion of **Casino Pier** collapsed into the ocean due to intense waves, with all of its roller coasters damaged, and a haunted house washed ashore nine miles away.

The **Star Jet roller coaster** fell off the damaged pier into the ocean but remained largely intact. Most of the rides in these amusement parks were destroyed, including roller coasters.

Governor Christie issued a mandatory evacuation for Long Beach Island on October 28, 2012, and residents and business owners were prohibited from returning until November 10, 2012. The island's estimated monetary damage was over $750 million.

Approximately two dozen oceanfront houses in Mantoloking were completely removed from their foundations and destroyed.

As of May 18, homeowners of Ortley Beach still had not been allowed onto the Barrier Island to check on their properties. Ortley Beach was declared "Ground Zero" because of the unbelievable amount of devastation.

In Keansburg, the storm washed 3 feet of sand into **Keansburg Amusement Park.**

Hurricane Sandy forced the Sandy Hook section of **Gateway National Recreation Area** to close for six months.

The **Belmar boardwalk** was also destroyed.

Photo Questions and Answers

1. What landmark is this on the Asbury Park Boardwalk?

2. What part of the Jersey Shore can you find a Capybara?

3. What popular beachside landmark, adjacent to the boardwalk, is this?

4. Why is this church in Long Branch called the Church of the Presidents?

5. Who is the Earl of Perth?

6. What is this   building?

7. Whose house was this?

8. Where can you find this six-story elephant?

9. Where can this character be found?

10. What was this ferry slip once fundamental for?

11. What is this?

12. What famous artist lived here?

13. Where is this beautiful lighthouse?

14. What is the story **behind this monument?**

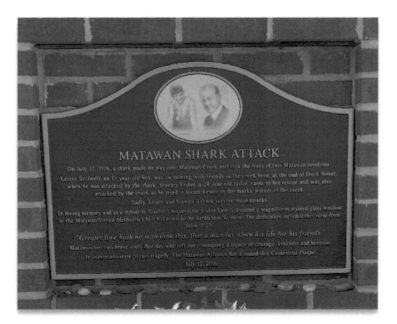

15. What is the story behind this beachfront property?

16. Which beach can you find this "Turtle Crossing" sign at the Jersey Shore?

17. Where can you find these twin lighthouses?

18. Why is this picture of Fred Astaire painted on the side of a building in Keyport?

19. Where is this 63-year-old arcade located?

20. What is this history behind the dolphins on this Ortley Beach water tower?

Photo Answers

1. Asbury Park Convention center, built between 1928 and 1930, and used for sports, concerts, and other special events.

2. Cape May County Park and Zoo, Cape May.

3. The Carousel House, Asbury Park.

4. The Church of the Presidents is a former Episcopal chapel on the Jersey Shore where seven United States presidents worshipped. It was visited by presidents Ulysses S. Grant, Rutherford B. Hayes, James A. Garfield, Chester A. Arthur, Benjamin Harrison, William McKinley, and Woodrow Wilson.

5. James Drummond, aka Lord Perth, was a partner with William Penn in the settlement of East New Jersey in 1681. As one of the 24 proprietors of a large parcel of property that took up much of what is now the State of New Jersey, Perth sponsored an expedition in 1684 to establish a settlement there.

    The City of Perth Amboy, which sits on the waterfront facing Staten Island, and which was once a port city in its own right, is named in his honor. The statue of Lord Perth stands in front of City Hall.

6. The Great Auditorium, in Ocean Grove, was constructed in 1894 and is mostly unchanged. Famed conductor, Leonard Bernstein, once compared it to Carnegie Hall.

7. One of the oldest standing houses in the city of Asbury Park — and the only surviving residence in the United States that boasts a direct association with the celebrated author of "The Red Badge of Courage" — the historic Stephen Crane House serves as the headquarters of the Asbury Park Historical Society, the nonprofit

organization that has welcomed thousands of visitors to the one-time home of the 19th century novelist, journalist, short story writer and poet.

8. Lucy the Elephant is an example of novelty architecture, constructed of wood and tin sheeting in 1881 by James V. Lafferty in Margate City.

9. This is just one of the characters that make up a mini-golf course on Seaside Heights Boardwalk.

10. The Perth Amboy Ferry Slip was once a vital ferry slip for boats in New York Harbor. It was restored in 1998 to its 1904 appearance.

11. The Propriety House in Perth Amboy is the only proprietary governor's mansion of the original Thirteen Colonies still standing. Construction was completed in 1764.

12. The Rockwell Cottage, now a private residence, was once a summer home where painter Norman Rockwell stayed with his family.

13. Sandy Hook

14. To honor victims of the 1916 shark attacks, which occurred in the Matawan community, in a creek two miles from the Raritan Bay. The over 300-pound bull shark was caught two days after the killings.

The bull shark is the only shark that can survive in both fresh and saltwater. This story partly inspired Peter Benchley to write the book, "Jaws."

15. "The Sinatra House" was the residence of the late Paul R. Smith, a former Sony Music Distribution chairman and an enormous fan of Frank Sinatra's music and voice. Smith decided to share his love with other people by playing his idol's songs through outdoor speakers on his property, a tradition that his children do their best to keep alive ever since Smith passed away in 2002.

16. Sandy Hook

17. Atlantic Highlands

18. Fred Astaire made his vaudeville debut with his older sister, Adele, in Keyport in 1905 at the young age of 6.

19. This family-owned establishment can be found on the boardwalk of Seaside Heights.

20. The dolphins were designed by Gregg Gordijn, a local artist. Gordijn won a contest sponsored by the Ortley Beach Sea-Bay Club in 1993. For his efforts he received a $100 savings bond, and his design was painted on the water tower for all to see.

Why People Love the Jersey Shore

The Jersey Shore is a beloved destination for beach-goers from all over the world. Here are 15 reasons why people love the beaches and communities along the Jersey Shore:

1. Miles of pristine coastline with plenty of room to spread out and enjoy the sun, sand, and surf.

2. A wide variety of beach towns, each with its own unique character and charm.

3. Endless activities like swimming, fishing, boating, and more.

4. Delicious seafood restaurants serving up fresh catches from local waters.

5. Quaint boardwalks lined with shops, arcades, rides, and more for family fun.

6. Beautiful Victorian architecture in some of the oldest beach towns like Cape May and Ocean Grove.

7. Historic lighthouses that have been guiding ships since colonial times.

8. Picturesque views of the Atlantic Ocean from high points like Sandy Hook or Island Beach State Park.\

9. Relaxing spas offering massages and other treatments to help you unwind after a day at the beach or exploring town attractions.

10. Festivals throughout the summer months celebrating music, art, food, culture, and more!

11. Unique wildlife such as dolphins playing in the waves or ospreys soaring overhead in search of their next meal.

12. The chance to explore nature trails or take a kayak tour through some of New Jersey's most beautiful waterways.

13. Abundant opportunities for surfing, paddle boarding, kiteboarding, sailing, windsurfing and other water sports.

14. Friendly locals who are always happy to share their favorite spots or give advice on where to find the best seafood around town!

15. A great place to relax, reconnect with friends and family, make new memories, or just get away from it all!

Hidden Gems

If you're planning a trip to the Jersey Shore, you might be wondering what hidden gems await you. We've done the research and found some of the best kept secrets on the Jersey Shore:

1. Sunset Beach: This secluded beach in Lower Township is known for its stunning sunsets and unique "Cape May diamonds" - smooth quartz stones that wash up on shore.

2. Cold Spring Village: Step back in time at this living history museum, where costumed actors bring 19th century life to life.

3. Naval Air Station Wildwood: This former military base has been transformed into a museum showcasing vintage aircraft and military artifacts.

4. Cape May Lighthouse: Climb to the top of this historic lighthouse for panoramic views of the coast.

5. Secret Jersey Shore book: For even more insider tips, check out "Secret Jersey Shore: A Guide to the Weird, Wonderful, and Obscure" by Mary Dixon Lebeau.

Most Popular Destination

The most popular destination on the Jersey Shore is undoubtedly Wildwood. It boasts a beautiful beach, clean boardwalk with fun attractions and delicious food, and plenty of lively nightlife venues. The town also has a historic district with quaint shops to explore, as well as iconic 1960s architecture that can be found up and down its main streets. In addition, Wildwood is a great spot for outdoor activities like fishing, surfing, bike riding along the shoreline, kayaking in nearby rivers or lakes, camping trips to nearby state parks and more! All of these factors make it one of the most popular coastal spots in New Jersey.

Most Popular Beaches

While there isn't a clear answer to what is the most popular beach on the Jersey Shore, here are some of the top picks:

1. Point Pleasant Beach - This beach is known for its family-friendly atmosphere and boardwalk attractions.

2. Stone Harbor - This beach is praised for its clean and well-maintained facilities, as well as its picturesque scenery.

3. Spring Lake - This beach offers a quieter and more relaxed atmosphere compared to other Jersey Shore beaches.

4. Ocean City - This beach is another family-friendly option with a long boardwalk and plenty of activities for all ages.

5. Cape May City Beaches - These beaches are known for their Victorian architecture and charming small-town feel.

6. Sandy Hook - This beach is located within a national park and offers stunning views of New York City across the water.